BULENT 60s

1964

**Other books in the
Turbulent 60s series:**

1960
1961
1962
1963
1965
1966
1967
1968
1969

THE TURBULENT 60s

1964

Kristin Rencher and Barbara Schuetze, *Book Editors*

Bonnie Szumski, *Publisher*
Scott Barbour, *Managing Editor*
David M. Haugen, *Series Editor*

GREENHAVEN
PRESS ®

THOMSON

GALE

San Diego • Detroit • New York • San Francisco • Cleveland
New Haven, Conn. • Waterville, Maine • London • Munich

© 2004 by Greenhaven Press. Greenhaven Press is an imprint of The Gale Group, Inc., a division of Thomson Learning, Inc.

Greenhaven® and Thomson Learning™ are trademarks used herein under license.

For more information, contact
Greenhaven Press
27500 Drake Rd.
Farmington Hills, MI 48331-3535
Or you can visit our Internet site at http://www.gale.com

Cover credit: © Bettmann/CORBIS
Library of Congress, 37, 44, 49, 61, 93, 102, 123
National Archives, 56, 87, 105

LIBRARY OF CONGRESS CATALOGING-IN-PUBLICATION DATA

1964 / Kristin Rencher and Barbara Schuetze, book editors.
    p. cm. — (The turbulent 60s)
Includes bibliographical references and index.
ISBN 0-7377-1500-6 (lib. bdg. : alk. paper) —
ISBN 0-7377-1501-4 (pbk. : alk. paper)
    1. United States—History—1961–1969—Sources. 2. Nineteen sixty-four, A.D.—Sources. I. Title: Nineteen sixty-four. II. Rencher, Kristin and Schuetze, Barbara. III. Series.
E846.A17 2004
973.923—dc21
                                                            2003054000

Printed in the United States of America

CONTENTS

Foreword   8

Introduction: The Year of Disillusionment   10

1. On Smoking and Health
by the Advisory Committee to the Surgeon General   18
The first surgeon general's report on "Smoking
and Health" was released on January 11, 1964,
linking smoking to lung cancer and
emphysema.

2. Direct Hit
by Newsweek   27
On February 3, with U.S. and Soviet tensions at
an all-time high, filmmaker Stanley Kubrick released *Dr. Strangelove*, a dark comedy that par-
odies the insane possibility of global nuclear
war.

3. The Beatles Invade America
by Alfred G. Aronowitz   31
On February 9, 1964, millions of American
teens tuned in for the Beatles' first appearance
on the *Ed Sullivan Show*.

4. The Birth of Muhammad Ali
by Mike Marqusee   41
Cassius Clay, the future Muhammad Ali, made
sports history when he beat Sonny Liston to become World Heavyweight Champion on February 25, 1964.

5. The Great Society and Johnson's War on Poverty
by Lyndon B. Johnson   46
President Johnson declared a "War on Poverty"

in his first State of the Union address on January 8, 1964. His declaration was the beginning of a social agenda that eventually became known as the "Great Society."

6. The Civil Rights Movement: "A Fraud, a Sham, and a Hoax"
by George C. Wallace   53

The landmark Civil Rights Act of 1964 was signed into law on July 3, 1964. The next day Governor George C. Wallace of Alabama gave a historic speech renouncing the legislation.

7. The Harlem Riot of 1964
by Paul L. Montgomery   65

Despite the passage of the Civil Rights Act of 1964, racial unrest continued unabated. Tempers flared and the formerly peaceful demonstrations against police turned violent.

8. Travels with the Merry Pranksters
by Paul Perry   72

In the summer of 1964 author Ken Kesey and his friends, who called themselves the Merry Pranksters, embarked on a cross-country trip in a psychedelic school bus.

9. Mississippi—"Everybody's Scared"
by Newsweek   77

Students from across the country headed to Mississippi for the "Freedom Summer." Their goal was to expand black voter registration, teach reading and math to black children, and aid indigent blacks.

10. The Lie That Launched Vietnam: The Tonkin Gulf Incident
Part I by Lyndon B. Johnson; Part II by Tom Wells   83

On August 4, President Johnson stated that the North Vietnamese had attacked U.S. Navy vessels in Vietnam's Tonkin Gulf. Within days Congress had passed a joint resolution support-

ing military action to prevent further
aggression.

11. The Free Speech Movement
by David Burner   90
By 1964, changing social mores and increasing
student activism on college campuses created a
clash with conservative educators and the business community.

12. The Warren Report
Part I by William H. Stringer;
Part II by the Warren Commission   98
A controversial report made public on Septem-
ber 27, 1964 rejected conspiracy theories and
maintained that Lee Harvey Oswald was solely
responsible for the assassination of President
John F. Kennedy.

13. The 1964 Election: Johnson, Goldwater, and "The Daisy Advertisement"
by Kathleen Hall Jamieson   112
During the 1964 presidential election, the John-
son campaign ran a television commercial, referred to as "The Daisy Advertisement," which
preyed on Cold War fears and painted opponent
Barry Goldwater as a warmonger.

14. Martin Luther King Jr. Wins Nobel Peace Prize
Part I by Gunnar Jahn;
Part II by Martin Luther King Jr.   121
In December 1964 Martin Luther King Jr. was
announced the winner of that year's Nobel
Peace Prize, firmly cementing the civil rights
leader's position as a champion for peace and
racial equality.

Chronology   128
For Further Research   133
Index   138

FOREWORD

The 1960s were a period of immense change in America. What many view as the complacency of the 1950s gave way to increased radicalism in the 1960s. The newfound activism of America's youth turned an entire generation against the social conventions of their parents. The rebellious spirit that marked young adulthood was no longer a stigma of the outcast but rather a badge of honor among those who wanted to remake the world. And in the 1960s, there was much to rebel against in America. The nation's involvement in Vietnam was one of the catalysts that helped galvanize young people in the early 1960s. Another factor was the day-to-day Cold War paranoia that seemed to be the unwelcome legacy of the last generation. And for black Americans in particular, there was the inertia of the civil rights movement that, despite seminal victories in the 1950s, had not effectively countered the racism still plaguing the country. All of these concerns prompted the young to speak out, to decry the state of the nation that would be their inheritance.

The 1960s, then, may best be remembered for its spirit of confrontation. The student movement questioned American imperialism, militant civil rights activists confronted their elders over the slow progress of change, and the flower children faced the nation's capitalistic greed and conservative ethics and opted to create a counterculture. There was a sense of immediacy to all this activism, and people put their bodies on the line to bring about change. Although there were reactionaries and conservative holdouts, the general feeling was that a united spirit of resistance could stop the inevitability of history. People could shape their own destinies, and together they could make a better world. As sixties chronicler Todd Gitlin writes, "In the Sixties it seemed especially true that History with a capital H had come down to earth, either interfering with life or making it possible: and that within History, or threaded through it, people were living with a supercharged density: lives were bound up with one another, making claims on one another, drawing one another into the common project."

Perhaps not everyone experienced what Gitlin describes, but few would argue that the nation as a whole was left untouched by the radical notions of the times. The women's movement, the civil rights movement, and the antiwar movement left indelible marks. Even the hippie movement left behind a relaxed morality and a more ecological mindset. Popular culture, in turn, reflected these changes: Music became more diverse and experimental, movies adopted more adult themes, and fashion attempted to replicate the spirit of uninhibited youth. It seemed that every facet of American culture was affected by the pervasiveness of revolution in the 1960s, and despite the diversity of rebellions, there remained a sense that all were related to, as Gitlin puts it, "the common project."

Of course, this communal zeitgeist of the 1960s is best attributed to the decade in retrospect. The 1960s were not a singular phenomenon but a progress of individual days, of individual years. Greenhaven Press follows this rubric in The Turbulent Sixties series. Each volume of this series is devoted to the major events that define a specific year of the decade. The events are discussed in carefully chosen articles. Some of these articles are written by historians who have the benefit of hindsight, but most are contemporary accounts that reveal the complexity, confusion, excitement, and turbulence of the times. Each article is prefaced by an introduction that places the event in its historical context. Every anthology is also introduced by an essay that gives shape to the entire year. In addition, the volumes in the series contain time lines, each of which gives an at-a-glance structure to the major events of the topic year. A bibliography of helpful sources is also provided in each anthology to offer avenues for further study. With these tools, readers will better understand the developments in the political arena, the civil rights movement, the counterculture, and other facets of American society in each year. And by following the trends and events that define the individual years, readers will appreciate the revolutionary currents of this tumultuous decade—the turbulent sixties.

The Year of Disillusionment

The dawn of 1964 was greeted by a nation still in mourning over the recent assassination of its charismatic young president, John F. Kennedy. Televised images of Kennedy's shooting as well as the horrific live broadcast of assassin Lee Harvey Oswald Jr. being shot to death by Dallas resident Jack Ruby left the nation numb and disillusioned. Kennedy's successor, former vice president Lyndon Baines Johnson, had been sworn in as president on November 22, 1963, in the hours following Kennedy's death. Just seven weeks later, on January 8, 1964, Johnson delivered his first State of the Union address as president of the United States.

Johnson, who first rose to national power in the late 1930s, was a protégé of Democratic president Franklin Delano Roosevelt. Although he would later criticize some of Roosevelt's policies, he was, like the rest of the country, enamored of the man who courageously led the country through the Great Depression. Johnson deeply admired Roosevelt's political savvy and had run his first successful congressional campaign on Roosevelt's New Deal platform in 1937. Hearkening back to New Deal optimism was the root of Johnson's political success and many public welfare programs were initiated in his first full year as president of the United States.

The Great Society

The lanky Texan set out in the New Year with a plan to revive the spirit of the New Deal. Johnson's idea was to draw the people together under a common goal, much as Roosevelt did during the Great Depression. Roosevelt's New Deal initiatives, which included Social Security and the Works Progress Administration, created a public safety net and put millions of unemployed Americans to work. Johnson wanted to create his own version of the New Deal to bring the nation out from under the shadow of Kennedy's death and to make his own unique mark on history.

Johnson's intent was to honor Kennedy's memory by furthering that administration's political and social initiatives while at the same time expanding their scope to encompass his own administration's social agenda. Kennedy programs such as the Peace Corps and the space program would be fully supported and joined by new initiatives. Johnson announced his first plan during the State of the Union address when he declared a war on poverty. Historian Robert H. Bremner called the war on poverty a "stirring call to arms" that the country embraced along with its "many-faceted programs designed 'to wipe out that shameful poverty' persisting in the midst of wealth."[1] Much of the spotlight was on rural poverty, especially in the Appalachians, but over half of the poverty facing the nation in 1964 was urban and tied to race.

As the year proceeded, Johnson continued to rally disheartened Americans by increasing the scope of the war on poverty to encompass a grand dream of a "Great Society" of American prosperity. In his speech to the graduating class at the University of Michigan, Johnson stated, "For in your time we have the opportunity to move not only toward the rich society and the powerful society, but upward to the Great Society. The Great Society rests on abundance and liberty for all. It demands an end to poverty and racial injustice, to which we are totally committed in our time. But that is just the beginning."[2]

Johnson's commitment to end racial injustice and his support of the civil rights movement were hallmarks of his presidency. However, they sometimes put him at odds with his southern heritage and constituency. Racism, which was often at the core of both urban and rural poverty, was part of the fabric of life in the South. When Johnson publicly signed the Civil Rights Act on national television on July 2, 1964—an event designed to bring the country together—conservative southerners became convinced that he was a traitor to their long-held traditions. It is a paradox that an occasion designed to unify the country for the betterment of all people served to polarize it instead. This is just one of the many ironies that history came to consider as fundamental to both the administration and the man.

The 1964 Election

Famed novelist Ralph Ellison, author of *Invisible Man*, once called Johnson the "greatest American president ever for the poor and the Negroes."[3] In fact, the support of African Americans was one of the keys to Johnson's successful presidential campaign that year. In 1964's summer of discontent—filled with demonstrations, race riots, cross burnings, and the murder of three civil rights workers in Mississippi—Johnson became a source of hope for many African Americans. Shortly after Harlem, the mostly black neighborhood in New York, was ravaged by riots in July, influential African American leaders, such as the Reverend Dr. Martin Luther King Jr. and Bayard Rustin, the March on Washington coordinator, called on their constituency to rally behind the president in his race against the Republican challenger, Arizona senator Barry Goldwater. Goldwater was perceived as a racist by most African Americans.

Johnson won the election by a landslide, aided by an unprecedented use of television advertising. In those ads Johnson implied that a vote for Goldwater was a vote for nuclear war. But despite the sensationalism of the advertising, the 1964 election was fought mostly on idealistic issues. Johnson's idealism, reminiscent of elections during the Roosevelt years, was a further effort to lift the spirits of the country. Ideals such as free speech, civil rights, and an end to poverty and racism were all topics for debate. During this time the terms *extremism* and *moderation* became political buzzwords. Goldwater, in his speech accepting the Republican nomination for president, stated, "I would remind you that extremism in the defense of liberty is no vice. And let me remind you also that moderation in the pursuit of justice is no virtue." Johnson responded to Goldwater by saying, "Extremism in the pursuit of the Presidency is an unpardonable vice. Moderation in the affairs of the nation is the highest virtue."[4]

Extremism

Despite Johnson's proclamation of moderation, 1964 will largely be remembered for extremism. Extreme politics, people, and events played major roles that year. From deadly riots in New York to militant students marching for free speech in Berkeley, California, disturbing images were in the spotlight on the nightly news. Even comedic entertainment reached a new level of extremism that was disconcerting to middle America; the obscenity-laden "sick" comedy of Lenny Bruce was so provocative that it resulted in his being censored and jailed. He was booked on obscenity charges in several cities across the country, bringing media attention to the cause of free speech. On June 14, 1964, one hundred prominent artists signed a statement that Bruce's arrest in New York City violated constitutional guarantees of free speech. In their statement, the artists said, "Whether we regard Bruce as a moral spokesman or simply as an entertainer, we believe he should be allowed to perform free from censorship or harassment." One of the signers stated, "I just don't think the police should be empowered to censor words. It's a matter of principle."[5]

While extremism existed at many levels, it was most evident in the civil rights arena. White racists such as the Ku Klux Klan and Alabama governor George Wallace often took center stage, but self-proclaimed black racist and Muslim cleric Malcolm X also made the news. Malcolm X (formerly Malcolm Little) had a profound impact on the black community, especially on young blacks who were dissatisfied with the slow rate of social change. He had one particularly effective and vocal proponent: boxer Cassius M. Clay. Clay, who became world heavyweight boxing champ in February 1964, publicly proclaimed his support of Islam, Malcolm X, and black separatism. Inspired by Malcolm X, Clay changed his middle initial to "X" shortly after winning the world title. He later changed his name once again, to Muhammad Ali.

Slow Progress of Civil Rights

Malcolm X was perhaps the most disillusioned American of all—so disillusioned that he did not even truly consider himself an American, although he was born in Omaha, Nebraska, in America's heartland. Malcolm X believed that violence was sometimes necessary in a fight for a cause and was in radical opposition to Martin Luther King Jr., who advocated peaceful, nonviolent means to end racism. In Malcolm X's "Ballot or Bullet" speech, given on April 3, 1964, he declared,

> Whether you're educated or illiterate, whether you live on the boulevard or in the alley, you're going to catch hell just like I am. We're all in the same boat and we all are going to catch the same hell from the same man. He just happens to be a white man. All of us have suffered here, in this country, political oppression at the hands of the white man, economic exploitation at the hands

of the white man, and social degradation at the hands of the
white man.

While King and his supporters advocated political action, using
"the ballot" as a means of effecting change, Malcolm X suggested
that there may be a time and a place for "the bullet."[6]

The rhetoric of Malcolm X was deeply disturbing to many
Americans but no more so than in the South, where many white
people were fearful of change and full of hatred for those who
wished to impose that change upon them. Their hatred was man-
ifested in the actions of the Ku Klux Klan during Mississippi's
Freedom Summer, when three civil rights workers were violently
murdered and then unceremoniously buried in an earthen dam.
The media and the Federal Bureau of Investigation descended
upon Philadelphia, Mississippi, that summer, putting the town
under a microscope. The people of the region were resentful of
outsiders scrutinizing their ways. Alabama governor George Wallace, who declared himself a Democratic presidential candidate
against Johnson in the 1964 race, spoke for embittered southern
whites during that time when he called the new Civil Rights Act
"a fraud, a sham and a hoax."[7]

Cultural Change
In 1964, established social behaviors were questioned, but the
world was changing in other ways as well. Rock and roll was here
to stay and the "British Invasion" had begun. Hailing from Liverpool, England, the Beatles came to America in the early part of the
year. Their live debut on *The Ed Sullivan Show* was viewed by what
was then the largest television audience in history, and the tour that
followed was equally record breaking. Shortly after their debut, another young British band, the Rolling Stones, fronted by lead singer
Mick Jagger, arrived in the United States. While the Stones were
not as big as the Beatles, their legacy—and longevity—have been
profound.

The Beatles and the Rolling Stones had a huge cultural impact
but, musically speaking, the year might be best typified by a song
released by folksinger Bob Dylan in January 1964. "The Times
They Are A-Changin'" was a lyrically sophisticated political
statement that was uncannily predictive of the course of social
and political change through the rest of the decade. The song not
only acknowledged and predicted change, but insisted upon it.

By the late 60s, "The Times They Are A-Changin'" became the anthem of social and political demonstrators everywhere. It was a call to action heeded by those who were disenchanted with the status quo.

Vietnam

Social and cultural changes were in abundance yet American opinion often remained conservative. While President Johnson was absolutely committed to social changes at home, he also strongly believed in the use of military force to advance the goals of U.S. foreign policy. It was an unquestioned tradition. At that time, U.S. foreign policy was defined by the Cold War; American's primary objective was to keep communism at bay and make the world safe for democracy. While there were lessons to be learned from the country's recent experience battling communism in Korea, no one was really listening—except for two senators from the Pacific Northwest.

Senators Wayne Morse of Oregon and Ernest Gruening of Alaska were the only critics when President Johnson came to Congress on August 5, 1964, after the U.S. Navy had been allegedly attacked by the Communist North Vietnamese in the Gulf of Tonkin. Since any aggressive Communist move was perceived as a threat, Johnson asked Congress to support his resolution to strike back at North Vietnamese targets. Morse objected on constitutional grounds. Article I of the Constitution gives Congress the power to declare war; he believed that Congress would surrender that power with the passage of the Gulf of Tonkin Resolution. With his dissenting vote, Morse stated, "I believe that within the next century, future generations will look with dismay and great disappointment upon a Congress which is now about to make such a historic mistake."[7] The rest of Congress was not persuaded. With only Morse and Gruening voting against the resolution, Congress helped propel America into one of its longest and bloodiest wars.

At the time, the morality of action against Vietnam was nearly unquestioned. Newspaper editorials across the country celebrated the Johnson administration's policy. And yet it eventually became obvious that something was horribly wrong. While Johnson had a grand and glorious presidential victory in 1964, it would be his only one. By 1968 a sense of foreboding had gripped some military advisers as well as a large section of the public. The Vietnam

War had become a disaster; millions of dollars and thousands of lives had been lost with no significant military success and no victory in sight. Public opinion had turned against continued involvement in Vietnam. Mired in controversy over the war, Johnson astounded the country in March 1968 by announcing that he would withdraw his bid for reelection. And so the man who advocated moderation would be taken down by military extremism.

Hope Remained

There is no doubt that the events of 1964 contributed to the country's sense of disillusionment. The evening news overflowed with stories of civil rights killings, race riots, student uprisings, and communism. And yet there was an underlying current of optimism. From the war on poverty to the Great Society, President Johnson worked tirelessly to inspire the people of the nation, and in many ways he succeeded. Idealistic young students continued to venture out as volunteers for the Peace Corps and civil rights causes, with great expectations of making the world a better place. The U.S. space program continued to move forward with the inspirational challenge of exploring the final frontier of space. And, most importantly, with the passage of the Civil Rights Act of 1964 came the dawn of a new age of racial equity.

As always, hope remained. At the end of the year, Martin Luther King Jr. was awarded the Nobel Peace Prize. At the age of thirty-five, he was the youngest person to receive the honor. In accepting the award, he brought an added dimension of promise to the year's struggles: "When years have rolled past and when the blazing light of truth is focused on this marvelous age in which we live—men and women will know and children will be taught that we have a finer land, a better people, a more noble civilization—because these humble children of God were willing to suffer for righteousness' sake." In the waning days of a year marked by both optimism and strife, King ended his speech by testifying that "the beauty of genuine brotherhood and peace is more precious than diamonds or silver or gold,"[8] leaving his audience to recognize that only unity and peace could bring about the needed changes in the country, in the world.

Notes

1. Robert H. Bremner, "The War on Poverty, 1964–1968." www.lexisnexis.com/academic/2upa/Aph/JohnsonPoverty.asp.

2. Lyndon B. Johnson, "The Great Society" speech, May 22, 1964.

3. Ralph Ellison, *Going to the Territory.* New York: Random House, 1986, p. 87.

4. Quoted in Robert Dallek, *Flawed Giant: Lyndon Johnson and His Times, 1961– 1973.* New York: Oxford University Press, 1998, p. 133.

5. Quoted in Thomas Buckley, "100 Fight Arrest of Lenny Bruce," *New York Times*, June 14, 1964.

6. Malcolm X, "The Ballot or the Bullet" speech, April 3, 1964.

7. Quoted in Mason Drukman, *Wayne Morse: A Political Biography.* Portland: Oregon Historical Society Press, 1997, p. 413.

8. Martin Luther King Jr., "1964 Nobel Peace Prize Acceptance Speech," December 10, 1964.

On Smoking and Health

By the Advisory Committee to the Surgeon General

The first surgeon general's report on "Smoking and Health" was re-leased on January 11, 1964, by the advisory committee of the U.S. Public Health Service and Surgeon General Luther Terry, M.D. Two years earlier the British Royal College of Physicians had released their own groundbreaking report, also called "Smoking and Health." It was the first concerted scientific and government effort to explore a possi-ble connection between smoking and disease. Both the U.S. and British reports reached similar conclusions about the hazards of smok-ing. The excerpts of the surgeon general's report that follow show there to be a causal link between smoking and lung cancer. Subsequent re-search and reports have continued to support those findings. The ulti-mate warning of the report advised that "Cigarette smoking is a health hazard of sufficient importance in the United States to warrant appro-priate remedial action."

In response to the report and in an effort to protect the American public, the Federal Trade Commission (FTC) quickly released new rules for cigarette advertising. The rules, which are still in effect today, were established as follows:

- Require clear product warnings on every package stating that ciga-rette smoking is dangerous to health.
- Ban all advertising that states or implies that smoking promotes good health or physical well-being.
- Prohibit advertisements which assert that one brand of cigarette is

Advisory Committee to the Surgeon General of the Public Health Service, *Smoking and Health*. Washington, DC: U.S. Department of Health, Education, and Welfare, January 11, 1964.

less harmful than another unless the claim is substantiated in advance.

Cigarette sales plummeted after the release of the report but, thanks to intensive public relations and advertising by the tobacco industry, sales returned to prior levels of growth by year's end. In fact, by the end of the following year tobacco product sales had reached an all-time high. The industry's success was achieved in part because of efforts to keep the public from perceiving that a definitive conclusion had been reached regarding the dangers of smoking. As part of this effort, the industry embarked on cooperative research projects with the American Cancer Society and the American Medical Association among others. The purported goal of the projects was to find conclusive evidence of the health risks, but its real effect was to keep the question open to public debate.

I n previous studies, the use of tobacco, especially cigarette smoking, has been causally linked to several diseases. Such use has been associated with increased deaths from lung cancer and other diseases, notably coronary artery disease, chronic bronchitis, and emphysema. These widely reported findings, which have been the cause of much public concern over the past decade, have been accepted in many countries by official health agencies, medical associations, and voluntary health organizations.

The potential hazard is great because these diseases are major causes of death and disability. In 1962, over 500,000 people in the United States died of arteriosclerotic heart disease (principally coronary artery disease), 41,000 died of lung cancer, and 15,000 died of bronchitis and emphysema. . . .

Another cause for concern is that deaths from some of these diseases have been increasing with great rapidity over the past few decades.

Lung cancer deaths, less than 3,000 in 1930, increased to 18,000 in 1950. In the short period since 1955, deaths from lung cancer rose from less than 27,000 to the 1962 total of 41,000. This extraordinary rise has not been recorded for cancer of any other site. While part of the rising trend for lung cancer is attributable to improvements in diagnosis and the changing age-composition and size of the population, the evidence leaves little doubt that a true increase in lung cancer has taken place.

Deaths from arteriosclerotic, coronary, and degenerative heart disease rose from 273,000 in 1940, to 396,000 in 1950, and to 578,000 in 1962.

Reported deaths from chronic bronchitis and emphysema rose from 2,300 in 1945 to 15,000 in 1962.

The changing patterns and extent of tobacco use are a pertinent aspect of the tobacco-health problem.

Nearly 70 million people in the United States consume tobacco regularly. Cigarette consumption in the United States has increased markedly since the turn of the Century, when per capita consumption was less than 50 cigarettes a year. Since 1910, when cigarette consumption per person (15 years and older) was 138, it rose to 1,365 in 1930, to 1,828 in 1940, to 3,322 in 1950, and to a peak of 3,986 in 1961. The 1955 Current Population Survey showed that 68 percent of the male population and 32.4 percent of the female population 18 years of age and over were regular smokers of cigarettes.

In contrast with this sharp increase in cigarette smoking, per capita use of tobacco in other forms has gone down. Per capita consumption of cigars declined from 117 in 1920 to 55 in 1962. Consumption of pipe tobacco, which reached a peak of 2½ lbs. per person in 1910, fell to a little more than half a pound per person in 1962. Use of chewing tobacco has declined from about four pounds per person in 1900 to half a pound in 1962.

The background for the Committee's study thus included much general information and findings from previous investigations which associated the increase in cigarette smoking with increased deaths in a number of major disease categories. It was in this setting that the Committee began its work to assess the nature and magnitude of the health hazard attributable to smoking.

Kinds of Evidence

In order to judge whether smoking and other tobacco uses are injurious to health or related to specific diseases, the Committee evaluated three main kinds of scientific evidence:

1. *Animal experiments.*—In numerous studies, animals have been exposed to tobacco smoke and tars, and to the various chemical compounds they contain, Seven of these compounds (polycyclic aromatic compounds) have been established as cancer-producing (carcinogenic). Other substances in tobacco and smoke, though not carcinogenic themselves, promote can-

cer production or lower the threshold to a known carcinogen. Several toxic or irritant gases contained in tobacco smoke produce experimentally the kinds of non-cancerous damage seen in the tissues and cells of heavy smokers. This includes suppression of ciliary action that normally cleanses the trachea and bronchi, damage to the lung air sacs, and to mucous glands and goblet cells which produce mucus.

2. *Clinical and autopsy studies.*—Observations of thousands of patients and autopsy studies of smokers and non-smokers show that many kinds of damage to body functions and to organs, cells, and tissues occur more frequently and severely in smokers. Three kinds of cellular changes—loss of ciliated cells, thickening (more than two layers of basal cells), and presence of atypical cells—are much more common in the lining layer (epithelium) of the trachea and bronchi of cigarette smokers than of non-smokers. Some of the advanced lesions seen in the bronchi of cigarette smokers are probably premalignant. Cellular changes regularly found at autopsy in patients with chronic bronchitis are more often present in the bronchi of smokers than non-smokers. Pathological changes in the air sacs and other functional tissue of the lung (parenchyma) have a remarkably close association with past history of cigarette smoking.

3. *Population studies.*—Another kind of evidence regarding an association between smoking and disease comes from epidemiological studies.

In retrospective studies, the smoking histories of persons with a specified disease (for example, lung cancer) are compared with those of appropriate control groups without the disease. For lung cancer alone, 29 such retrospective studies have been made in recent years. Despite many variations in design and method, all but one (which dealt with females) showed that proportionately more cigarette smokers are found among the lung cancer patients than in the control populations without lung cancer.

Extensive retrospective studies of the prevalence of specific symptoms and signs—chronic cough, sputum production, breathlessness, chest illness, and decreased lung function—consistently show that these occur more often in cigarette smokers than in non-smokers. Some of these signs and symptoms are the clinical expressions of chronic bronchitis, and some are associated more with emphysema; in general, they increase with amount of smoking and decrease after cessation of smoking.

Another type of epidemiological evidence on the relation of smoking and mortality comes from seven prospective studies which have been conducted since 1951. In these studies, large numbers of men answered questions about their smoking or non-smoking habits. Death certificates have been obtained for those who died since entering the studies, permitting total death rates and death rates by cause to be computed for smokers of various types as well as for non-smokers. The prospective studies thus add several important dimensions to information on the smoking-health problem. Their data permit direct comparisons of the death rates of smokers and nonsmokers, both overall and for individual causes of death, and indicate the strength of the association between smoking and specific diseases. . . .

Findings of the Prospective Studies

In general, the greater the number of cigarettes smoked daily, the higher the death rate. For men who smoke fewer than 10 cigarettes a day, according to the seven prospective studies, the death rate from all causes is about 40 percent higher than for non-smokers. For those who smoke from 10 to 19 cigarettes a day, it is about 70 percent higher than for non-smokers; for those who smoke 20 to 39 a day, 90 percent higher; and for those who smoke 40 or more, it is 120 percent higher.

Cigarette smokers who stopped smoking before enrolling in the seven studies have a death rate about 40 percent higher than non-smokers, as against 70 percent higher for current cigarette smokers. Men who began smoking before age 20 have a substantially higher death rate than those who began after age 25. Compared with non-smokers, the mortality risk of cigarette smokers, after adjustments for differences in age, increases with duration of smoking (number of years), and is higher in those who stopped after age 55 than for those who stopped at an earlier age.

In two studies which recorded the degree of inhalation, the mortality ratio for a given amount of smoking was greater for inhalers than for non-inhalers.

The ratio of the death rates of smokers to that of non-smokers is highest at the earlier ages (40–50) represented in these studies, and declines with increasing age. . . .

The array of information from the prospective and retrospective studies of smokers and non-smokers clearly establishes an association between cigarette smoking and substantially higher death rates. . . .

In this inquiry the epidemiologic method was used extensively in the assessment of causal factors in the relationship of smoking to health among human beings upon whom direct experimentation could not be imposed. Clinical, pathological, and experimental evidence was thoroughly considered and often served to suggest an hypothesis or confirm or contradict other findings. When coupled with the other data, results from the epidemiologic studies can provide the basis upon which judgments of causality may be made.

It is recognized that no simple cause-and-effect relationship is likely to exist between a complex product like tobacco smoke and a specific disease in the variable human organism. It is also recognized that often the coexistence of several factors is required for the occurrence of a disease, and that one of the factors may play a determinant role; that is, without it, the other factors (such as genetic susceptibility) seldom lead to the occurrence of the disease. . . .

The Committee's Judgment in Brief

On the basis of prolonged study and evaluation of many lines of converging evidence, the Committee makes the following judgment:

Cigarette smoking is a health hazard of sufficient importance in the United States to warrant appropriate remedial action. . . .

Cancer by Site

Lung Cancer: Cigarette smoking is causally related to lung cancer in men; the magnitude of the effect of cigarette smoking far outweighs all other factors. The data for women, though less extensive, point in the same direction.

The risk of developing lung cancer increases with duration of smoking and the number of cigarettes smoked per day, and is diminished by discontinuing smoking.

The risk of developing cancer of the lung for the combined group of pipe smokers, cigar smokers, and pipe and cigar smokers, is greater than for non-smokers, but much less than for cigarette smokers. The data are insufficient to warrant a conclusion for each group individually.

Oral Cancer: The causal relationship of the smoking of pipes to the development of cancer of the lip appears to be established.

Although there are suggestions of relationships between cancer of other specific sites of the oral cavity and the several forms of tobacco use, their causal implications cannot at present be stated.

Cancer of the Larynx: Evaluation of the evidence leads to the judgment that cigarette smoking is a significant factor in the causation of laryngeal cancer in the male.

Cancer of the Esophagus: The evidence on the tobacco-esophageal cancer relationship supports the belief that an association exists. However, the data are not adequate to decide whether the relationship is causal.

Cancer of the Urinary Bladder: Available data suggest an association between cigarette smoking and urinary bladder cancer in the male but are not sufficient to support a judgment on the causal significance of this association.

Stomach Cancer: No relationship has been established between tobacco use and stomach cancer.

Non-Neoplastic Respiratory Diseases

Cigarette smoking is the most important of the causes of chronic bronchitis in the United States, and increases the risk of dying from chronic bronchitis.

A relationship exists between pulmonary emphysema and cigarette smoking but it has not been established that the relationship is causal. The smoking of cigarettes is associated with an increased risk of dying from pulmonary emphysema.

For the bulk of the population of the United States, the importance of cigarette smoking as a cause of chronic bronchopulmonary disease is much greater than that of atmospheric pollution or occupational exposures.

Cough, sputum production, or the two combined are consistently more frequent among cigarette smokers than among non-smokers.

Cigarette smoking is associated with a reduction in ventilatory function. Among males, cigarette smokers have a greater prevalence of breathlessness than non-smokers.

Cigarette smoking does not appear to cause asthma.

Although death certification shows that cigarette smokers have a moderately increased risk of death from influenza and pneumonia, an association of cigarette smoking and infectious diseases is not otherwise substantiated.

Cardiovascular Disease

Smoking and nicotine administration cause acute cardiovascular effects similar to those induced by stimulation of the autonomic nervous system, but these effects do not account well for the observed association between cigarette smoking and coronary disease. It is established that male cigarette smokers have a higher death rate from coronary disease than non-smoking males. The association of smoking with other cardiovascular disorders is less well established. If cigarette smoking actually caused the higher death rate from coronary disease, it would on this account be responsible for many deaths of middle-aged and elderly males in the United States. Other factors such as high blood pressure, high serum cholesterol, and excessive obesity are also known to be associated with an unusually high death rate from coronary disease. The causative role of these factors in coronary disease, though not proven, is suspected strongly enough to be a major reason for taking countermeasures against them. It is also more prudent to assume that the established association between cigarette smoking and coronary disease has causative meaning than to suspend judgment until no uncertainty remains.

Male cigarette smokers have a higher death rate from coronary artery disease than non-smoking males, but it is not clear that the association has causal significance.

Other Conditions

Peptic Ulcer: Epidemiological studies indicate an association between cigarette smoking and peptic ulcer which is greater for gastric than for duodenal ulcer.

Tobacco Amblyopia: Tobacco amblyopia (dimness of vision unexplained by an organic lesion) has been related to pipe and cigar smoking by clinical impressions. The association has not been substantiated by epidemiological or experimental studies.

Cirrhosis of the Liver: Increased mortality of smokers from cirrhosis of the liver has been shown in the prospective studies. The data are not sufficient to support a direct or causal association.

Maternal Smoking and Infant Birth Weight: Women who smoke cigarettes during pregnancy tend to have babies of lower birth weight.

Information is lacking on the mechanism by which this decrease in birth weight is produced.

It is not known whether this decrease in birth weight has any influence on the biological fitness of the newborn.

Smoking and Accidents: Smoking is associated with accidental deaths from fires in the home.

No conclusive information is available on the effects of smoking on traffic accidents. . . .

Psychosocial Aspects of Smoking

A clear cut smoker's personality has not emerged from the results
so far published. While smokers differ from non-smokers in a variety of characteristics, none of the studies has shown a single
variable which is found solely in one group and is completely ab-
sent in another. Nor has any single variable been verified in a sufficiently large proportion of smokers and in sufficiently few non-
smokers to consider it an "essential" aspect of smoking.

The overwhelming evidence points to the conclusion that
smoking—its beginning, habituation, and occasional discontin-
uation—is to a large extent psychologically and socially determined. This does not rule out physiological factors, especially in
respect to habituation, nor the existence of predisposing constitutional or hereditary factors.

Direct Hit

By *Newsweek*

The satiric film *Dr. Strangelove, or: How I Learned to Stop Worrying and Love the Bomb*, commonly referred to as *Dr. Strangelove*, is a popular classic directed by distinguished filmmaker Stanley Kubrick, who also wrote the screenplay. When it was released in early 1964, the film created a sensation because of its black humor and irreverent view of the "evil" system of science and technology in the atomic age.

According to Kubrick, he originally intended a serious treatment of his theme: the accidental launching of a nuclear warhead and the resulting Soviet-American cooperation to keep war from ensuing. But as he delved into the material, he decided the subject better lent itself to a black comedy, a total satire on the Cold War and the madness of the nuclear arms race between the United States and the USSR. The events of the film take place after the 1962 Cuban Missile Crisis, in which the United States and the Soviet Union came close to a nuclear war. The movie was upsetting because of the very real possibility of nuclear annihilation, but it captured people's imaginations with its farcical perspective.

Dr. Strangelove won a number of "best film" awards and has been placed in the National Film Registry of the Library of Congress. The National Film Registry, part of the National Film Preservation Act of 1988, is meant to preserve up to twenty-five "culturally, historically, or aesthetically significant films" each year. The historic significance of *Dr. Strangelove* earned it the distinction of being among the first films chosen for the National Film Registry.

An unnamed staff writer for *Newsweek* wrote the following review of the film. The article, entitled "Direct Hit," was published in the magazine's February 3, 1964, issue to coincide with the movie's release.

I t is outrageous, of course. The President of the United States of America is named Merkin Muffley. The Premier of Russia is Dimitri Kissof and the ambassador is de Sadesky. The commander of Burpelson Air Force Base is Gen. Jack D. Ripper. There is a Col. "Bat" Guano. But outrageous, excessive, and nearly insane is exactly what Stanley Kubrick wanted to be in DR. STRANGELOVE OR: HOW I LEARNED TO STOP WORRYING AND LOVE THE BOMB.

The story is that of the end of the world. Ripper is a maniac, a rightist fanatic who is worried about the Commie plot to put fluoride in our drinking water and debilitate us by interfering with the "purity of our body fluids." This ought to sound impossibly stupid, and it does, but it also has an uncomfortably familiar ring. Ripper takes it upon himself to bomb the Soviet Union, which is something that hardly bears thinking about, but which Kubrick makes perfectly plausible.

"Strangelove" throughout is all too plausible. As Kubrick says: "The greatest message of the film is in the laughs. You know, it's true! The most realistic things are the funniest."

In a weird way, he is perfectly right. It is hilarious to watch Peter Sellers as President Muffley talking to Kissof on the phone and getting into an argument with Kissof about which one of them is sorrier for what has happened. It is uproarious when the SAC fliers in the B-52 go over their survival kits: money in rubles, dollars, and gold, Benzedrine, cigarettes, nylons, chocolate, chewing gum, prophylactics, tranquilizers, and so on ("I could have a pretty fine weekend with this in Vegas," one of the fliers remarks a bit ruefully.)

Or there is Sellers again, this time as Ripper's adjutant, Group Captain Mandrake, the only man in the world who knows the code that must be used to recall the bomber. He must call the President. There is a phone booth. But the White House doesn't accept collect calls from unknown group captains. He tells "Bat" Guano to shoot off the lock from a Coke machine for the 55 cents, but Guano, in shock and horror says: "That's private property!"

This is low clowning, of course, but it suggests all too clearly that human society is not yet so well organized as to be able to afford such dangerous toys as hydrogen bombs.

Even the discussion about the probable war and the possible end of the world is ridiculous *because* it is so familiar. George C. Scott, as Gen. "Buck" Turgidson, is in favor of sending the rest of the planes to knock the Reds off the map. Their retaliatory force, he says will be reduced so that the U.S. will suffer "only acceptable casualties—ten to twenty megadeaths," and he adds with a sporting shrug, "depending on the breaks." It is crazy. It is fantastic and obscene. The idea of 20 million deaths and the word that makes an abstraction out of it are both simply ridiculous.

That Stanley Kubrick has had the nerve to say so, and that he has said it in a comedy, which makes it all the sharper, all the clearer, and that much better a film, is truly fine. Kubrick, and his biting bitter satire, stands as eloquent testimony not only to the possibilities of intelligent comment in film, but to the great freedom which moviemakers have, even if most of them have not dared use it. That thundering "No" is thrilling to see on the screen.

It is also side-splittingly funny. At its very worst, even at the grim moment of truth, Kubrick keeps his nerve and drops the bomb, with Slim Pickens riding it down to doom like a cowboy riding a bronco—with a wild wave of his stupid Stetson and a yell of sheer exaltation that turns imperceptibly but surely into a cry of pure terror, without the slightest change in timbre, volume, or pitch. The edge of that yell is a razor's edge, and it cuts deep.

How Kubrick Did It

Stanley Kubrick does everything in his films except act. He finds a story, shapes the script, chooses all the actors, supervises the lighting and costumes, operates the cameras, directs the cast, edits the film, and then supervises the publicity. On "Strangelove," which was filmed without the cooperation of any government agency, he was also the sole military adviser, bringing to bear all his military experience—watching war movies at Loew's in New York.

Naturally, the picture was made without Pentagon help. The instrument-jammed B-52 cockpit was built from a picture in a British magazine. It cost $100,000. And each shot of the B-52 in flight, made with a 10-foot model and a moving matte, cost more than $6,000.

Such painstaking attention to every film-making detail is the natural result of Kubrick's whole approach to his subject. He did not just sit down and decide to make a comedy about the end of the world. Over a six-year period, just for his own edification, and at first with no idea of making a film, he devoured some 70 books on nuclear war, subscribed to *Missiles and Rockets*, *The Bulletin of the Atomic Scientists*, and a megaton of other magazines and pamphlets. One day he came across "Two Hours to Doom" (called "Red Alert" in the U.S.), a suspense novel about an Air Force general triggering off a nuclear holocaust, and decided that had to be his next movie.

Once committed, he never let up. "Kubrick has a fantastic drive," says novelist Terry Southern, who collaborated on the brilliant screenplay of "Strangelove." "He's got a weird metabolism; while I'm taking Dexamil, he's taking Seconal."

The book was dead serious, but the 34-year-old Kubrick found that each time he tried to create a scene, it came up funny. "How the hell could the President ever tell the Russian Premier to shoot down American planes?" he asked, with a broad wave of his hand. "Good Lord, it sounds ridiculous."

SRO

Actually Kubrick's chief concern now is fantasy, the sort of "nightmare comedy" that "Red Alert" came to be. "The real image doesn't cut the mustard, doesn't transcend," he says. "I'm now interested in taking a story, fantastic and improbable, and trying to get to the bottom of it, to make it seem not only real, but inevitable."

"Dr. Strangelove," filmed with the backing and the blessing of Columbia Pictures, cost $1.5 million, and, as Southern says, "If anyone submitted the script cold to a major studio, the reaction would be, 'Are you kidding?'"

Kubrick can now call his own shots, but how can you top a movie about total annihilation? He is fascinated by outer space, which he thinks is inhabited, and he is reading and reading and reading about it. Or, "I can always do a story about overpopulation," says Kubrick. "Do you realize that in 2020 there will be no room on earth for all the people to stand? The really sophisticated worriers are worried about that."

The Beatles Invade America

By Alfred G. Aronowitz

By 1963, fans in Europe were already buying millions of Beatles records, dressing like the British rock stars, and sporting moplike Beatles haircuts. At concerts, girls went wild, screaming and fainting over the Fab Four: John Lennon, Paul McCartney, George Harrison, and Ringo Starr.

When the Beatles arrived in New York on February 7, 1964, they were likewise greeted by thousands of wildly screaming fans and a horde of journalists, photographers, radio stations, and TV crews. The reception was unprecedented and the buzz generated was dubbed "Beatlemania."

Within forty-eight hours, the Beatles made their historic performance on the *Ed Sullivan Show*. Due to an incredible blitz of preshow publicity, a record-breaking 73 million viewers tuned in to watch them. Thousands of screaming fans fell in love with the four lads from Liverpool, England. The Beatles' February 9, 1964, appearance on Sullivan's popular weekly variety show has been rated as the top moment for rock and roll in television history.

To what did the Beatles owe their phenomenal fame in America? Many factors came together to create the Fab Four's success. Prior to the Beatles' arrival, a massive publicity campaign generated momentum. And the time was ripe for a diversion after the somber period following President John F. Kennedy's assassination in November 1963. The Beatles offered an exciting new sound that appealed to young people. And importantly, the Beatles were creative and excellent musicians who expanded the boundaries of rock and roll.

However, some thought the Beatles were simply a passing fad. Even Ed Sullivan's musical director reportedly said, "I give them a year." Their detractors were wrong. The Beatles have changed the face of popular music forever and influenced an entire generation.

Rock journalist Alfred G. Aronowitz captures the Beatles' incredible power to send waves of teenagers into emotional frenzy in his *Saturday Evening Post* article "The Beatles: Music's Gold Bugs." The article appeared in the March 21, 1964 issue of the magazine, a little more than a month after the Beatles' first appearance on the *Ed Sullivan Show*.

Brian Sommerville is a balding 32-year-old Londoner whose jaw juts out like the southeast corner of England when he thinks he is about to say something important. At Kennedy International Airport in New York last February 7 [1963], Sommerville's jaw was projecting so far he was almost unable to open his mouth to speak. A thousand screaming teen-agers were trying to wriggle toward a thin white line of a nylon rope that had been stretched across the terminal building lobby. Three thousand more were screaming from behind bulging metal railings atop the roof, where they were the guests of New York disc jockeys, who had invited them to take the day off from school.

Next to Sommerville a New York *Journal-American* photographer was tugging angrily at his arm, shouting, "We bought an exclusive story and we can't even get a picture of them looking at us—what did we pay you money for?" At Sommerville's other arm a phalanx of British correspondents was complaining that the police wouldn't let them into the press room. There wasn't space left in the press room anyway, and one of the cops tried to throw out a Capitol Records executive who had arrived without an identification badge. Disc jockeys equipped with tape recorders were pointing cylindrical microphones at the mob. Flashbulbs exploded. From the back of the lobby came word that two girls had fainted. Hemmed in and harassed, Sommerville's jaw signaled a pronouncement. "This," he said in the intonations of a nation that has been accustomed to ruling the world, "has gotten entirely out of control." Sommerville is press officer of a rock-'n'-roll group known as the Beatles. Their plane had just landed.

Four Young Britons

Amid a fanfare of screeches, there emerged for young Britons in Edwardian four-button suits. One was short and thick-lipped. Another was handsome and peach-fuzzed. A third had a heavy face and the hint of buck-teeth. On the fourth, the remnants of adolescent pimples were noticeable. Their names were Ringo Starr, Paul McCartney, John Lennon and George Harrison, but they were otherwise indistinguishable beneath their manes of mop-like hair.

After they were ushered into the floodlit uproar of the press room, Brian Sommerville, acting as master of ceremonies, stepped to a microphone, again thrust out his jaw and addressed the reporters. "Gentlemen, gentlemen, gentlemen," he said, "will you please shut up!" The first question from the American press was, "Do you believe in lunacy?" "Yeah," answered one of the Beatles, "it's healthy." Another reporter asked, "Would you please sing something?" "No," replied another Beatle, "we need money first." Still another reporter asked, "Do you hope to take anything home with you!" "Yeah," a Beatle replied, "Rockefeller Center." At first, few of the reporters could remember which Beatle was which. But by the end of their two-week visit to America, each of them had become a distinct personality. Each of them, in fact, had become a star.

Ringo

Ringo is the one that some observers have compared to Harpo Marx. He has bright blue eyes that remind one of a child looking through a window, although he sometimes deliberately crosses them as he sits dumbly at the drums playing his corny four-four beat. "I hate phonies," he says with the absolutism of somebody who thinks he can spot one a mile away. "I can't *stand* them." The most popular of the Beatles in America, he evokes paroxysms of teen-age shrieks everywhere by a mere turn of his head, a motion which sends his brown spaniel hair flying. When he flips his wig, the kids flip theirs. *"RIIINNGO! RIIINNGO!"* the kids call out. He acquired the nickname because he wears two rings on each hand. He wears different rings at different times, changing them like cuff links. "I like the gold ones," he says. "The fans send a lot of silver ones, too, but I send them back." Then he adds, "Do you know I have 2,761 rings?" His fame has brought Ringo other treasures, but he seems not to have forgotten what it was like to grow up amid the grimy row-house streets of Liverpool.

He was born Richard Starkey, the only son of a father who was a house painter and a mother who was a barmaid. He never finished school. He was kept out by pleurisy and more than a dozen stomach operations. Also, it seems, he never started growing. Asked how tall he is, he snaps back. "Two feet, nine inches!" Actually he is five-feet-seven. "When I feel my head starting to swell," says John Lennon, "I just look at Ringo and I know perfectly well we're not supermen." Without proper schooling, Ringo worked as an electrician's apprentice and at various odd jobs before turning to drumming. . . .

He sits with his drums behind the group as the other three perform, and he rarely sings, although that is what he would most like to do. Although, at 23, he is the oldest of the Beatles, he is at the bottom of what sociologists would call their pecking order. When he joined the group it already had a record contract, and the unspoken feeling in the quartet is that Ringo was hired by the other three. When they disagree on anything, Ringo is the last to get his way. "You'd be nowhere," Paul McCartney says to him in the ultimate squelch, "if it weren't for the rest of us."

Paul

The fans call Paul the handsome one, and he knows it. The others in the group call Paul "The Star." He does most of the singing and most of the wiggling, trying to swing his hips after the fashion of Elvis Presley, one of his boyhood idols. In the British equivalent of high school, Paul was mostly in the upper ranks scholastically, unlike the other Beatles. "He was like, you know, a goody-goody in school," remembers one of Paul's boyhood friends. He also, as another former classmate remembers him, was a "tubby little kid" who avoided girlish rejections by avoiding girls.

He can afford to be much bolder now. At a cocktail party in the British embassy in Washington, a twice-divorced noblewoman put her arms around him, gazed longingly into his eyes and said, "Which one are you?" "Roger," he answered. "Roger what?" she said. "Roger McClusky the fifth," he answered, and slithered out of her grasp.

"Paul is the hardest one to get to know, although that doesn't mean he's the deepest," says a friend. When the 18-year-old English actress Jill Haworth had a private audience with Paul in Miami Beach, it lasted only a few minutes. "I just couldn't find any-thing to talk to him about," she later said. "It was just impossi-ble to get started talking."

Paul, who plays bass guitar, wears the same tight pants that are part of the uniform of the Beatles, although he often distin-guishes himself with a vest. "Paul," says one member of the troupe, "is the only one of the boys who's had it go to his head." Sometimes, talking with the other Beatles, he finds himself us-ing accents much more high-toned than the working-class slang of Liverpool, where he grew up. When he does, John Lennon mockingly mimics him.

Paul and John have collaborated in writing more than 100 songs, including such hits as *I Want to Hold Your Hand* and *She Loves You.* "None of us really knows how to read or write mu-sic," says Paul. "The way we work is like, we just whistle. John will whistle at me, and I'll whistle back at him."

John

John doesn't smile when he sings. "That's because," says Neil Aspinall, the 22-year-old road manager who grew up in Liver-pool with the Beatles, "he's giving you his soul." He likes to wear sunglasses both indoors and out, as a sort of declaration of pri-vacy. "John," says Brian Epstein, the 29-year-old personal man-ager who discovered the Beatles, "is the most intellectual of the boys." Though he has a habit of falling asleep at odd moments, he is also the most intense and has a temper that reddens his face at the slightest rub. . . .

John began with ideas of becoming a painter, spending two years at the Liverpool Art Institute. He also writes short stories and poems, a collection of which, combined with his sketches, is being published in London. One editor calls Lennon's literary efforts "British hip, a sort of conglomeration of funny Lewis Car-roll jabberwocky with a slight tinge of William Burroughs's *Naked Lunch* and an almost Joycean word play."

When John first appeared on *The Ed Sullivan Show*, a subtitle identifying him carried the parenthetical message, "Sorry, girls, he's married." His wife Cynthia is a quietly beautiful 21-year-old blonde whom he met at the Liverpool Art Institute and whom the newspapers now call, to the Lennons' disgust, "Mrs. Beatle." When the Beatles traveled from New York to Washington, she wore a black wig so she could get through the crowd. In Washington, she remained alone in her hotel room. In Miami Beach she sunbathed by herself. "Ever since the boys became famous," says Cynthia, "it's become more and more difficult for me to see John." They have an infant son, John, whom the newspapers call, again to their disgust, "Baby Beatle." When the Lennons have business visitors, Cynthia serves tea and recedes into the background. "Women," says John, "should be obscene and not heard."

John is the leader of the Beatles. "We *have* no leader," he might argue with some annoyance. "We're a *team*, y'know, pull together and all that." As a matter of fact, each Beatle has a veto on what the four of them do together. "But it's John who usually wins out," says one of their friends. "John is the hippest and the sharpest of the lot. They've all learned from him. Even their humor, the way they're always sending people up, they got that from John."

George

Just 22, George Harrison is the youngest of the Beatles. "He doesn't have the maturity of the others, so he tends to play it a little safe," says a member of the troupe. "It's as if he's the baby of the family." Being the baby of the family is a role to which George is accustomed. The son of a bus driver, he is the youngest of four children. "George was always the one who tried to please," says his sister, Mrs. Louise Caldwell, the pretty platinum-blond wife of an engineer who lives in the Midwest. "When the fire needed more coal, he would always say, 'Mummy, I'll do it, let me get the shovel.' Or when we'd be going to church, George would polish everyone's boots."

George plays lead guitar for the Beatles, often with a look of unconcern that seems to reflect a desire to be strumming elsewhere. "Well," he says, "the songs that Paul and John write, they're all right, but they're not the greatest.". . .

George's ambition, he says, is to retire with "a whacking great pile of money." He recalls that in the early days of the group in Liverpool, "we got what would work out to two dollars a night apiece—and all the soda we could drink. We drank until that stuff came out our ears to make sure we got our money's worth."

Little more than six months ago one of his major desires was to own a racing car. He now owns a Jaguar. Although by no means the quietest of the Beatles, because none of them really is quiet, George remains the least prominent. At a press conference for fan magazines in New York's Plaza Hotel, a young woman asked, "Mr. Starr is known for his rings, Mr. McCartney, obviously for his looks, and Mr. Lennon for his wife. What about you, Mr. Harrison!" George swallowed a bite of a chicken sandwich, fluttered his long eyelashes in the same manner that Paul often does and answered, "As long as I get an equal share of the money, I'm willing to stay anonymous."

Worldwide Beatlemania

These are the Beatles, the four young men who brought with them to America a phenomenon known as Beatlemania. So far, Beatlemania has traveled over two continents. In Stockholm the arrival of the Beatles was greeted with teen-age riots. In Paris another congregation held screeching services at the airport and the Beatles' performances at the Olympia Theater were sold out for three weeks. In the Beatles' native Liverpool 60 youngsters collapsed from exposure after standing all night in a mile-long line of 12,000 waiting to buy tickets to the Beatles' performance. When a foreman shut off the radio in the middle of a Beatles record at a textile mill in Lancashire, 200 girls went out on strike.

While the Beatles toured the United States, three of their singles were in the top six and their albums ranked one and two in the record popularity charts. Beatle wigs were selling at three dollars apiece, high-school boys were combing their forelocks forward and hairdressers were advertising Beatle cuts for women,

The Beatles wave to thousands of screaming fans after their arrival at Kennedy International Airport in New York City.

Beatle hats, T-shirts, cookies, eggcups, ice cream, dolls, beach shirts, turtleneck pullovers, nighties, socks and iridescent blue-and-green collarless suits were on the market, and a Beatle motor scooter for children and a Beatlemobile for adults were being readied for production. American bartenders were confounded by a sudden deluge of orders for Scotch and Coke, the Beatles' favorite drink. "I think everyone has gone daft," says John. Adds Ringo, "Anytime you spell beetle with an 'a' in it, we get the money." In 1964, Beatle-licensed products stand to gross $50 million in America alone. As for the Beatles, their total 1964 income is expected to reach $14 million.

It all began in Liverpool, a smog-aired, dockfront city that overlooks the Mersey River. When the Beatles first put their brows together eight years ago, there were an estimated 100 rock-'n'-roll groups in the city. Today Liverpool is the pop music capital of the British Isles, and what newspapers have come to call "The Mersey Sound" dominates the English hit parade. "Do you want to know what the Mersey sound is?" says one American critic. "It's 1956 American rock bouncing back at us."

Beatle History

In the beginning the group was called the Quarrymen Skiffle Group, then the Moondogs and then the Moonshiners. John, Paul and George were in the original group; Ringo Starr joined in 1962. Hired in 1959 for a job in Hamburg, Germany, the Beatles worked their way up to a wage of $25 a week, and became one of the main attractions along the Reeperbahn, the main street of the city's red-light district.

"When they got back to Liverpool, that's when they really started to swing," says Neil Aspinall. It was then that Brian Epstein discovered them. A delicately mannered young man who once wanted to be a dress designer, Epstein at the time was in charge of the television-radio-records department of his father's department-store chain. When several customers began demanding Beatles records, Epstein signed them up, got them a test with Decca Records, which they flunked, and then brought them to Electric and Musical Industries Ltd. . . .

In the United States, Capitol Records, which has first rights to any E.M.I. release, originally turned down the Beatles' records. As the craze grew it not only issued them but poured $50,000 into a promotion campaign. "Sure there was a lot of hype," says

Capitol vice president Voyle Gilmore. "But all the hype in the world isn't going to sell a bad product."

American Reception

Nevertheless, that hype helped stir the interest of thousands of fans who greeted the Beatles at Kennedy Airport. Many thousands more waited for them at New York's Plaza Hotel. Outside the hotel, stacked up against barricades the mob chanted. *"We want the Beatles! We want the Beatles!"* According to one maid, the Beatles found three girls hiding in their bathtub. Dozens of others climbed the fire exit to the 12th-floor wing in which the Beatle entourage had been ensconced. Still others, with the names and pocketbooks of prominent families, checked in at the hotel and tried to get to the Beatles via the elevators.

On the 12th floor the Beatles rested in their suite while the phones rang with requests for interviews and autographs. One call was from a man who wanted to produce Beatle ashtrays. Another was from a promoter in Hawaii who wanted to book the Beatles.

Telegrams came in by the handful, and boxes loaded with fan mail. "We get 12,000 letters a day," Ringo later said. "Yeah," added John. "We're going to answer every one of them." The road managers, meanwhile, were busy signing the Beatles' autographs for them, and the room-service waiters kept bringing up tables loaded with Scotch, ice and bottles of Coke. Murray the K also came in, bringing with him the Ronettes, an American recording group of three exotic looking girls. "We met the Beatles in Europe," one of them said, as if she were singing it.

As the Beatles' stay at the Plaza extended, so did the throngs. Each time the Beatles left the hotel, the mobs would break through police lines in a jumble of lost shoes, falling girls and Beatle sweat shirts. A deputy chief inspector of police accused the Beatles' press agents of bringing in teen-agers by the busload. The Beatles, meanwhile, spent their time watching TV, dining at the "21" Club, sightseeing from their car, twisting at the Peppermint Lounge, and flirting with bunnies in the Playboy Club.

The Tour

The remainder of the Beatles' tour of America was more of the same. In Washington, to which the Beatles traveled aboard a private railroad car called The King George, 2,000 teen-age fans mobbed the locked metal gates of Union Station. At their concert in the Coliseum that night the Beatles were showered with flashbulbs, hair rollers, caramels and jelly beans, in some instances a bagful at a time. "M' God!" Ringo said afterward. "They *hurt*. They felt just like hailstones."

When they flew to Miami, they were greeted at the airport by a chimpanzee, four bathing beauties, a four-mile-long traffic jam and 7,000 teen-agers, who shattered 23 windows and a plate-glass door. The flight-engineer of the plane wore a Beatle wig. As they were getting off, the wife of the president of National Airlines came aboard with two teen-age girls, but was blocked by Sommerville, who stormed, *"No, no, madam!* We cannot spend time giving autographs to employees' families." At the Deauville Hotel, they were hustled into an elevator. Along the way Ringo recognized a girl singer and pulled her into the elevator. Later a reporter asked Ringo who she was. "She's just a girl I know," he said. "What's her last name?" the reporter asked. "I don't know her *that* well," Ringo answered.

In Miami Beach the Beatles went yachting, swam in a private pool, posed for photographs on the beach while an elderly woman kept walking deliberately in front of the cameras, and then visited the training camp of Cassius Clay.

At one point, Sommerville, beaming with gratitude, decided to thank the police sergeant in charge of the Beatles' security detail by offering him a compliment. "Somebody told me," Sommerville said warmly, "that Miami Beach has the best police department that money can buy." Upstairs in Sommerville's room John was busy answering the telephone, with the calls again coming, one after the other, from as far away as Hawaii. "Hallooo," he said. "Brian Slummerfield here. . . . Yes luv. . . . Yes luv. . . . No luv. . . . G'by luv."

The Beatles flew back to England on February 21 to make their first movie. When they stopped off at Kennedy Airport to change planes for London, they again found several thousand teen-age fans screaming from the observation roof after waiting there for hours. Four girls collapsed. When it was all over, America could relax—at least, until the Beatles return this summer.

The Birth of Muhammad Ali

By Mike Marqusee

They called him "The Greatest" because that is what he called himself. Cassius X. Clay burst onto the sports scene with a dramatic victory over Sonny Liston, capturing the World Heavyweight Boxing Championship in February 1964. He won the fight in the eighth round, proving his own predictions correct, but soon after the fight he was making headlines for more than his athletic prowess. His religion, his politics, his friends, and his ideology were all front page news.

People considered Clay a brash and brazen young man. Civil rights activists were especially wary of Clay. On one hand, he was the embodiment of black pride and a source of hope for the black community. On the other, he was a potential threat. His adoption of the Islamic faith and his association with the Black Muslims, a group that advocated separation of the races, and its spokesman Malcolm X, made more moderate activists worry that he would derail their work toward the goal of social integration and racial equality.

In his book *Redemption Song: Muhammad Ali and the Spirit of the Sixties* journalist, social activist, and author Mike Marqusee chronicles Clay's transformation into a cultural icon. As the year progressed Clay adopted a new religion, changed his name to Muhammad Ali, and reaffirmed his heavyweight championship title by defeating Sonny Liston in a rematch. The controversy that surrounded the man would not be confined to 1964. Ali would continue to make headlines for many years, including in 1966 when he refused induction into the military as

Mike Marqusee, *Redemption Song: Muhammad Ali and the Spirit of the Sixties*. London: Verso, 1999. Copyright © 1999 by Mike Marqusee. Reproduced by permission.

a conscientious objector. His quote, "I ain't got no quarrel with them Vietcong" set off a firestorm of public debate that ultimately ended with his being stripped of his world heavyweight title.

On 25 February 1964, Cassius Clay defeated Sonny Liston to become heavyweight champion of the world. This against-the-odds victory was one of the shocking upheavals characteristic of the era, a surprise that compelled people to reconsider their assumptions. The triumph of the underdog, and with it the confounding of bookmakers and experts, is one of the most visceral thrills sports have to offer; it brings with it a combined sense of disorientation and unsuspected possibility, feelings which were to be intensified by Clay's actions outside the ring in the days that followed.

After the fight, Clay chose to forgo the usual festivities at one of Miami's luxury hotels and headed instead for the black ghetto, where he had made camp during training. He spent a quiet evening in private conversation with Malcolm X [minister and national spokesman for the Nation of Islam], the singer Sam Cooke and Jim Brown, the great Cleveland Browns running back and an early champion of black rights in sports. The next morning, after breakfast with Malcolm, Clay met the press to confirm the rumors that he was involved with the Nation of Islam:

> I believe in Allah and in peace. I don't try to move into white neighborhoods. I don't want to marry a white woman. I was baptized when I was twelve, but I didn't know what I was doing. I'm not a Christian any more. I know where I'm going, and I know the truth, and I don't have to be what you want me to be. I'm free to be what I want.

"I don't have to be what you want me to be." No boxing champion, and no black sports star, had ever issued such a ringing declaration of independence. The next day, Clay amplified his views. In place of his usual ingratiating bravado, there was now a steely and even exultant defiance:

Clay Becomes an Activist

> Black Muslims is a press word. The real name is Islam. That means peace. Islam is a religion and there are seven hundred and fifty million people all over the world who believe in it, and I'm

one of them. I ain't no Christian. I can't be when I see all the colored people fighting for forced integration get blowed up. They get hit by stones and chewed by dogs and they blow up a Negro church and don't find the killers. . . . I'm the heavyweight champion, but right now there are some neighborhoods I can't move into. I know how to dodge boobytraps and dogs. I dodge them by staying in my own neighborhood. I'm no trouble-maker . . . I'm a good boy. I never have done anything wrong. I have never been to jail. I have never been in court. I don't join any integration marches. I don't pay any attention to all those white women who wink at me. I don't carry signs. . . . A rooster crows only when it sees the light. Put him in the dark and he'll never crow. I have seen the light and I'm crowing.

Public Blacklash

Reactions to Clay's announcement were swift and hostile. The southern-dominated World Boxing Association (WBA) began moves to strip him of his title. His record album, *I Am the Greatest*, was pulled from the shelves by Columbia [Records]. A scheduled appearance on the Jack Parr "television talk" show was canceled. Endorsement deals evaporated. Senators threatened to mount an investigation into the legality of the Liston fight. The syndicate of Louisville millionaires who sponsored Clay described him as "ungrateful." With a fine disregard for history, Jimmy Cannon, the doyen of boxing writers, declared that boxing had never before "been turned into an instrument of mass hate. . . . Clay is using it as a weapon of wickedness." Harry Markson, the head of Madison Square Garden, warned Clay, "You don't use the heavyweight championship of the world to spout religious diatribe. We've made so much progress in eliminating color barriers that it's a pity we're now facing such a problem."

Joe Louis joined in the condemnation: "Clay will earn the public's hatred because of his connections with the Black Muslims. The things they preach are the opposite of what we believe." NAACP [National Association for the Advancement of Colored People] leader Roy Wilkins echoed the sentiment: "Cassius may not know it, but he is now an honorary member of the White Citizens' Councils. . . . He speaks their piece better than they do." [Boxer] Floyd Patterson told the press he would fight Ali for free "just to get the title away from the Black Muslims."

Other black voices struck a more realistic balance. "Consid-

Elijah Muhammad, leader of the Black Muslims, addresses an assembly of Muslim followers.

ering the associations and activities of other prizefighters I have known," observed George Schuyler, a conservative columnist, "Cassius Marcellus Clay is picking good company." Jackie Robinson [the first African American to play major league baseball] insisted, "Clay has as much right to ally himself with the Muslim religion as anyone else has to be a Protestant or a Catholic." Despite his sometimes "crude" behavior, Clay, Robinson believed, had "spread the message that more of us need to know: 'I am the Greatest,' he says. I am not advocating that Negroes think they are greater than anyone else. But I want them to know they are just as great as other human beings." And a younger man, [poet and black nationalist] Leroi Jones, saw even greater possibilities in the new champ: "Clay is not a fake, and even his blustering and playground poetry are valid; they demonstrate that a new and more complicated generation has moved onto the scene. And in this last sense Clay is definitely my man."

Clay's Transformation to Ali

Cassius Clay's conversion to the Nation of Islam set him on a path to uncharted lands, and transformed him in the eyes of both black and white. As a young challenger he had been brash and bold, an entertaining eccentric; within hours of winning the championship he had metamorphosed into an alien menace. He dared to turn his back on America, Christianity and the white race. Many black men had been lynched for less. The governors of American sports stood appalled as Clay brought the anarchy of political controversy into their orderly realm. Boxing fans were bemused. And in the black communities, while there was much dismay over Clay's rejection of the civil rights movement, there was also, among many, a mood of pleasant surprise. Whatever else it may have been, Clay's conversion to the Nation of Islam was recognized as an embrace of blackness; in willingly subjecting himself to the vilification that had been the lot of the Nation of Islam for years, he had placed his black constituency on a higher footing than the white audience to whom black performers were normally beholden, and this in itself earned him legions of black admirers.

"I'm free to be what I want." It's often said that at this moment Muhammad Ali "invented himself." Through sheer charisma he brought the old stereotypes tumbling down like a black Samson in the temple of the Philistines. But he did not invent himself out of nothing. In his search for personal freedom he was propelled and guided by a wide array of interacting social forces. Ali's public conversion was one of the unexpected jolts that peppered the decade, opening dizzying vistas of both fear and hope. But as with all such moments, its significance can only be discovered by diving into the river of historical experience which flows into and out from it.

The Great Society and Johnson's War on Poverty

By Lyndon B. Johnson

Lyndon B. Johnson's "War on Poverty" was announced in his first State of the Union address on January 8, 1964, with the words, "This administration today, here and now, declares unconditional war on poverty in America." It was an attempt to break a cycle that persisted in many parts of the country despite an economic expansion that had reduced the national unemployment rate to 5.3 percent. From Harlem to the Appalachia, poverty still gripped over 35 million Americans.

President Johnson took his proposal to Congress in March 1964. The War on Poverty had the following five basic components: 1) skill training through the creation of a Job Corps, a work-training program and a work study program, 2) a community action program designed to address regional solutions to the problem, 3) recruitment of volunteers to enact programs, 4) loans and guarantees as incentives to businesses that employ the unemployed, and 5) the creation of the Office of Economic Opportunity (OEO), which was designed to coordinate the mobilization of the nation's human and financial resources in an effort to combat poverty.

As the months passed, Johnson's utopian vision expanded beyond the scope of poverty to tackle medical care, civil rights, education, and affordable housing issues. By spring of 1964 Johnson had begun to re-

Lyndon B. Johnson, University of Michigan commencement address, May 22, 1964.

fer to his vision as "The Great Society." He presented it to the public for the first time in a speech to graduates of the University of Michigan that May. The Great Society exploded into the greatest burst of legislative activity since the New Deal of the 1930s, resulting in the creation of countless social programs including VISTA (Volunteers in Service to America), Neighborhood Youth Corps, Job Corps, College Work Study, and Head Start, as well as Medicare and Medicaid. The Great Society also encompassed the creation of the Office of Housing and Urban Development.

The Economic Opportunity Act was signed into law on August 20, 1964. However, funding for the OEO was never adequate and was further reduced as spending for the Vietnam War increased. It was one of many programs spawned by the Great Society that did not live up to expectations. Despite that, Johnson's vision and the resulting legislation achieved some reductions in poverty and, in fact, many Great Society social programs continue to this day.

I have come today from the turmoil of your Capital to the tranquility of your campus to speak about the future of your country.

The purpose of protecting the life of our Nation and preserving the liberty of our citizens is to pursue the happiness of our people. Our success in that pursuit is the test of our success as a Nation.

For a century we labored to settle and to subdue a continent. For half a century we called upon unbounded invention and untiring industry to create an order of plenty for all of our people.

The challenge of the next half century is whether we have the wisdom to use that wealth to enrich and elevate our national life, and to advance the quality of our American civilization.

Your imagination, your initiative, and your indignation will determine whether we build a society where progress is the servant of our needs, or a society where old values and new visions are buried under unbridled growth. For in your time we have the opportunity to move not only toward the rich society and the powerful society, but upward to the Great Society.

Vision of the Great Society

The Great Society rests on abundance and liberty for all. It demands an end to poverty and racial injustice, to which we are totally committed in our time. But that is just the beginning.

The Great Society is a place where every child can find knowledge to enrich his mind and to enlarge his talents. It is a place where leisure is a welcome chance to build and reflect, not a feared cause of boredom and restlessness. It is a place where the city of man serves not only the needs of the body and the demands of commerce but the desire for beauty and the hunger for community.

It is a place where man can renew contact with nature. It is a place which honors creation for its own sake and for what it adds to the understanding of the race. It is a place where men are more concerned with the quality of their goals than the quantity of their goods.

But most of all, the Great Society is not a safe harbor, a resting place, a final objective, a finished work. It is a challenge constantly renewed, beckoning us toward a destiny where the meaning of our lives matches the marvelous products of our labor.

So I want to talk to you today about three places where we begin to build the Great Society—in our cities, in our countryside, and in our classrooms.

Urban Renewal

Many of you will live to see the day, perhaps 50 years from now, when there will be 400 million Americans—four-fifths of them in urban areas. In the remainder of this century urban population will double, city land will double, and we will have to build homes, high-ways, and facilities equal to all those built since this country was first settled. So in the next 40 years we must rebuild the entire urban United States.

Aristotle said: "Men come together in cities in order to live, but they remain together in order to live the good life." It is harder and harder to live the good life in American cities today. The catalog of ills is long: there is the decay of the centers and the despoiling of the suburbs. There is not enough housing for our people or transportation for our traffic. Open land is vanishing and old landmarks are violated.

Worst of all, expansion is eroding the precious and time honored values of community with neighbors and communion with nature. The loss of these values breeds loneliness and boredom and indifference.

Our society will never be great until our cities are great. Today the frontier of imagination and innovation is inside those cities and not beyond their borders. New experiments are already going on. It will be the task of your generation to make the American city a place where future generations will come, not only to live but to live the good life.

I understand that if I stayed here tonight I would see that Michigan students are really doing their best to live the good life.

Lyndon B. Johnson's Great Society programs helped reduce poverty in the 1960s.

This is the place where the Peace Corps was started. It is inspiring to see how all of you, while you are in this country, are trying so hard to live at the level of the people.

Preserving Natural Splendor

A second place where we begin to build the Great Society is in our countryside. We have always prided ourselves on being not only America the strong and America the free, but America the beautiful. Today that beauty is in danger. The water we drink, the food we eat, the very air that we breathe, are threatened with pollution. Our parks are overcrowded, our seashores overburdened. Green fields and dense forests are disappearing.

A few years ago we were greatly concerned about the "Ugly American." Today we must act to prevent an ugly America.

For once the battle is lost, once our natural splendor is destroyed, it can never be recaptured. And once man can no longer walk with beauty or wonder at nature his spirit will wither and his sustenance be wasted.

The Promise of Education

A third place to build the Great Society is in the classrooms of America. There your children's lives will be shaped. Our society will not be great until every young mind is set free to scan the farthest reaches of thought and imagination. We are still far from that goal.

Today, 8 million adult Americans, more than the entire population of Michigan, have not finished 5 years of school. Nearly 20 million have not finished 8 years of school. Nearly 54 million—more than one-quarter of all America—have not even finished high school.

Each year more than 100,000 high school graduates, with proved ability, do not enter college because they cannot afford it. And if we cannot educate today's youth, what will we do in 1970 when elementary school enrollment will be 5 million greater than 1960? And high school enrollment will rise by 5 million. College enrollment will increase by more than 3 million.

In many places, classrooms are overcrowded and curricula are outdated. Most of our qualified teachers are underpaid, and many of our paid teachers are unqualified. So we must give every child a place to sit and a teacher to learn from. Poverty must not be a bar to learning, and learning must offer an escape from poverty.

But more classrooms and more teachers are not enough. We must seek an educational system which grows in excellence as it grows in size. This means better training for our teachers. It means preparing youth to enjoy their hours of leisure as well as their hours of labor. It means exploring new techniques of teaching, to find new ways to stimulate the love of learning and the capacity for creation.

Your Generation Must Lead

These are three of the central issues of the Great Society. While our Government has many programs directed at those issues, I do not pretend that we have the full answer to those problems.

But I do promise this: We are going to assemble the best thought and the broadest knowledge from all over the world to find those answers for America. I intend to establish working groups to prepare a series of White House conferences and meetings—on the cities, on natural beauty, on the quality of education, and on other emerging challenges. And from these meetings and from this inspiration and from these studies we will begin to set our course toward the Great Society.

The solution to these problems does not rest on a massive program in Washington, nor can it rely solely on the strained resources of local authority. They require us to create new concepts of cooperation, a creative federalism, between the National Capital and the leaders of local communities.

Woodrow Wilson once wrote: "Every man sent out from his university should be a man of his Nation as well as a man of his time."

Within your lifetime powerful forces, already loosed, will take us toward a way of life beyond the realm of our experience, almost beyond the bounds of our imagination.

For better or for worse, your generation has been appointed by history to deal with those problems and to lead America toward a new age. You have the chance never before afforded to any people in any age. You can help build a society where the demands of morality, and the needs of the spirit, can be realized in the life of the Nation.

So, will you join in the battle to give every citizen the full equality which God enjoins and the law requires, whatever his belief, or race, or the color of his skin? Will you join in the battle to give every citizen an escape from the crushing weight of poverty?

Will you join in the battle to make it possible for all nations to live in enduring peace—as neighbors and not as mortal enemies?

Will you join in the battle to build the Great Society, to prove that our material progress is only the foundation on which we will build a richer life of mind and spirit?

There are those timid souls who say this battle cannot be won; that we are condemned to a soulless wealth. I do not agree. We have the power to shape the civilization that we want. But we need your will, your labor, your hearts, if we are to build that kind of society.

Those who came to this land sought to build more than just a new country.

They sought a new world. So I have come here today to your campus to say that you can make their vision our reality. So let us from this moment begin our work so that in the future men will look back and say: It was then, after a long and weary way, that man turned the exploits of his genius to the full enrichment of his life.

The Civil Rights Movement: "A Fraud, a Sham, and a Hoax"

By George C. Wallace

In 1963 Martin Luther King Jr. had organized peaceful demonstrations in Birmingham, Alabama, to protest segregation in public facilities. Many whites responded angrily and violence erupted in the city. President John F. Kennedy was forced to place federal troops on alert and to warn Governor George C. Wallace that continued violence against peaceful civil rights marchers would bring the troops into action.

As the events unfolded, national news media brought them into American homes, showing images of whites beating African Americans and police using electric cattle prods to control the crowd. People across the country were outraged by what they saw and protested the senseless violence through letters to their congressmen. In many cities, African Americans expressed their outrage by rioting.

By 1964, a few months after Kennedy's assassination, it was clear that the deplorable social condition existing for African Americans required congressional legislation to correct. The result was the passage of the 1964 Civil Rights Act. Within a few hours of passage, President Lyndon Johnson signed the new act into law in a televised national broadcast from the White House with the following words:

> We believe that all men are created equal—yet many are denied equal treatment. We believe that all men have certain inalienable

George C. Wallace, speech in Atlanta, Georgia, July 4, 1964.

rights. We believe that all men are entitled to the blessings of liberty—yet millions are being deprived of those blessings, not because of their own failures, but because of the color of their skins.

The reasons are deeply embedded in history and tradition and the nature of man. We can understand without rancor or hatred how all this happens. But it cannot continue. Our Constitution, the foundation of our Republic, forbids it. The principles of our freedom forbid it. Morality forbids it. And the law I sign tonight forbids it.

Not all Americans responded favorably to the new law, especially in the South where the specter of change disrupted everyday lives and disturbed decades of accepted social practice. Alabama governor George C. Wallace spoke fervently for those who felt most threatened by the changes, as is shown by his speech delivered July 4, 1964. Besides arguing against federal policy, Wallace, in his speech, pledged his presidential candidacy. Wallace made a strong but failed run in 1968 and ran again in 1972 only to be felled by an assassin's bullet and paralyzed from the waist down. Years later, he recanted his racist beliefs and apologized to the African American community. Wallace's redemption was so complete that he was elected again as governor of Alabama in 1982 with the support of many African Americans.

We come here today in deference to the memory of those stalwart patriots who on July 4, 1776, pledged their lives, their fortunes, and their sacred honor to establish and defend the proposition that governments are created by the people, empowered by the people, derive their just powers from the consent of the people, and must forever remain subservient to the will of the people.

Today, 188 years later, we celebrate that occasion and find inspiration and determination and courage to preserve and protect the great principles of freedom enunciated in the Declaration of Independence.

It is therefore a cruel irony that the President of the United States has only yesterday signed into law the most monstrous piece of legislation ever enacted by the United States Congress.

It is a fraud, a sham, and a hoax.

This bill will live in infamy. To sign it into law at any time is tragic. To do so upon the eve of the celebration of our independence insults the intelligence of the American people.

It dishonors the memory of countless thousands of our dead who offered up their very lives in defense of principles which this bill destroys.

Never before in the history of this nation have so many human and property rights been destroyed by a single enactment of the Congress. It is an act of tyranny. It is the assassin's knife stuck in the back of liberty.

With this assassin's knife and a blackjack in the hand of the Federal force-cult, the left-wing liberals will try to force us back into bondage. Bondage to a tyranny more brutal than that imposed by the British monarchy which claimed power to rule over the lives of our forefathers under sanction of the Divine Right of kings.

Today, this tyranny is imposed by the central government which claims the right to rule over our lives under sanction of the omnipotent black-robed despots who sit on the bench of the United States Supreme Court. . . .

Mocking Our Freedom

To illustrate the fraud—it is not a Civil Rights Bill. It is a Federal Penal Code. It creates Federal crimes which would take volumes to list and years to tabulate because it affects the lives of 192 million American citizens. Every person in every walk and station of life and every aspect of our daily lives becomes subject to the criminal provisions of this bill.

It threatens our freedom of speech, of assembly, or association, and makes the exercise of these Freedoms a federal crime under certain conditions.

It affects our political rights, our right to trial by jury, our right to the full use and enjoyment of our private property, the freedom from search and seizure of our private property and possessions, the freedom from harassment by Federal police and, in short, all the rights of individuals inherent in a society of free men.

Ministers, lawyers, teachers, newspapers, and every private citizen must guard his speech and watch his actions to avoid the deliberately imposed booby traps put into this bill. It is designed to make Federal crimes of our customs, beliefs, and traditions. Therefore, under the fantastic powers of the Federal judiciary to punish for contempt of court and under their fantastic powers to regulate our most intimate aspects of our lives by injunction, every American citizen is in jeopardy and must stand guard against these despots.

Yet there are those who call this a good bill.

It is people like Senator Hubert Humphrey and other members of Americans for Democratic Action. . . .

We find Senator Hubert Humphrey telling the people of the United States that "nonviolent" demonstrations would continue to serve a good purpose through a "long, busy and constructive summer."

Yet this same Senator told the people of this country that passage of this monstrous bill would ease tensions and stop demonstrations.

This is the same Senator who has suggested, now that the Civil Rights Bill is passed, that the President call the fifty state Governors together to work out ways and means to enforce this rotten measure.

There is no need for him to call on me. I am not about to be a party to anything having to do with the law that is going to destroy individual freedom and liberty in this country.

I am having nothing to do with enforcing a law that will destroy our free enterprise system.

I am having nothing to do with enforcing a law that will destroy neighborhood schools.

Lyndon B. Johnson, a strong advocate for civil rights, is pictured signing the Civil Rights Bill of 1968.

I am having nothing to do with enforcing a law that will destroy the rights of private property.

I am having nothing to do with enforcing a law that destroys your right—and my right—to choose my neighbors—or to sell my house to whomever I choose.

I am having nothing to do with enforcing a law that destroys the labor seniority system.

I am having nothing to do with this so-called civil rights bill.

The liberal left-wingers have passed it. Now let them employ some pinknik [Communist sympathizer] social engineers in Washington, D.C., to figure out what to do with it. . . .

The Left-Wing Press

But I am not here to talk about the separate provisions of the Federal Penal Code. I am here to talk about principles which have been overthrown by the enactment of this bill. The principles that you and I hold dear. The principles for which our forefathers fought and died to establish and to defend. The principles for which we came here to rededicate ourselves.

But before I get into that, let me point out one important fact. It would have been impossible for the American people to have been deceived by the sponsors of this bill had there been a responsible American press to tell the people exactly what the bill contained. If they had had the integrity and the guts to tell the truth, this bill would never have been enacted.

Whoever heard of truth put to the worst in free and open encounter? We couldn't get the truth to the American people.

You and I know that that's extremely difficult to do where our newspapers are owned by out-of-state interests. Newspapers which are run and operated by left-wing liberals, Communist sympathizers, and members of the Americans for Democratic Action and other Communist front organizations with high sounding names.

However, we will not be intimidated by the vultures of the liberal left-wing press. We will not be deceived by their lies and distortions of truth. We will not be swayed by their brutal attacks upon the character and reputation of any honest citizen who dares stand up and fight for liberty. . . .

In this connection I want to pay my highest respects and compliments to the dedicated men of Atlanta and of Georgia who gave to the people of their state what is destined to become the true voice of the south. I have reference to the great newspaper the *Atlanta Times.*

It is a sad commentary on the period in which we live that it is necessary for the people of a great city to start their own newspaper in order to get the truth.

I hope you have some success in this venture and I assure you that there will be many subscribers in the State of Alabama including myself.

As I have said before, that Federal Penal Code could never have been enacted into law if we had had a responsible press who was willing to tell the American people the truth about what it actually provides. Nor would we have had a bill had it not been for the United States Supreme Court.

The Tyrannical Court

Now on the subject of the Court let me make it clear that I am not attacking any member of the United States Supreme Court as an individual. However, I do attack their decisions, I question their intelligence, their common sense and their judgment, I consider the Federal Judiciary system to be the greatest single threat to individual freedom and liberty in the United States today, and I'm going to take off the gloves in talking about these people.

There is only one word to describe the Federal judiciary today. That word is "lousy."

They assert more power than claimed by King George III, more power than Hitler, Mussolini, or Khrushchev ever had. They assert the power to declare unconstitutional our very thoughts. To create for us a system of moral and ethical values. To outlaw and declare unconstitutional, illegal, and immoral the customs, traditions, and beliefs of the people, and furthermore they assert the authority to enforce their decrees in all these subjects upon the American people without their consent. . . .

The only reason it [the U.S. Supreme Court] is the Supreme Law of the Land today is because we have a President who cares so little for freedom that he would send the armed forces into the states to enforce the dictatorial decree.

Our colonist forefather had something to say about that too.

The Declaration of Independence cited as an act of tyranny the fact that, ". . . Kept among us in times of peace standing armies without the consent of the legislature."

Today, 188 years later, we have actually witnessed the invasion of the State of Arkansas, Mississippi, and Alabama by the armed forces of the United States and maintained in the state against the will of the people and without consent of state legislatures.

It is a form of tyranny worse than that of King George III who had sent mercenaries against the colonies because today the Federal Judicial tyrants have sanctioned the use of brother against brother and father against son by federalizing the National Guard. . . .

It has reached the point where one may no longer look to judicial decisions to determine what the court may do. However, it is possible to predict with accuracy the nature of the opinions to be rendered. One may find the answer in the Communist Manifesto.

The Communists are dedicated to the overthrow of our form of government. They are dedicated to the destruction of the concept of private property. They are dedicated to the object of destroying religion as the basis of moral and ethical values.

The Communists are determined that all natural resources shall be controlled by the central government, that all productive capacity of the nation shall be under the control of the central government, that the political sovereignty of the people shall be destroyed as an incident to control of local schools. It is their objective to capture the minds of our youth in order to indoctrinate them in what to think and not how to think.

I do not call the members of the United States Supreme Court Communists. But I do say, and I submit for your judgment the fact that every single decision of the court in the past ten years which related in any way to each of these objectives has been decided against freedom and in favor of tyranny.

A politician must stand on his record. Let the Court stand on its record.

The record reveals, for the past number of years, that the chief, if not the only beneficiaries of the present Court's rulings, have been duly and lawfully convicted criminals, Communists, atheists, and clients of vociferous left-wing minority groups. . . .

The Court's Shameful Record

Let us look at the record further with respect to the court's contribution to the destruction of the concept of God and the abolition of religion.

The Federal court rules that your children shall not be permitted to read the bible in our public school systems.

Let me tell you this, though. We still read the bible in Alabama schools and as long as I am governor we will continue to read the bible no matter what the Supreme Court says.

Federal courts will not convict a "demonstrator" invading and destroying private property. But the Federal courts rule you cannot say a simple "God is great, God is good, we thank Thee for our food," in kindergartens supported by public funds.

Now, let us examine the manner in which the Court has continuously chipped away at the concept of private property. It is contended by the left-wing liberals that private property is merely a legal fiction. That one has no inherent right to own and possess property. The courts have restricted and limited the right of acquisition of property in life and have decreed its disposition in death and have ruthlessly set aside the wills of the dead in order to attain social ends decreed by the court. The court has substituted its judgment for that of the testator based on social theory.

The courts assert authority even in decree the use of private cemeteries.

They assert the right to convert a private place of business into a public place of business without the consent of the owner and without compensation to him.

One justice asserts that the mere licensing of a business by the state is sufficient to convert it into control by the Federal judiciary as to its use and disposition.

Another asserts that the guarantees of equal protection and due process of law cannot be extended to a corporation.

In one instance, following the edicts of the United States Supreme Court, a state Supreme Court has ordered and directed a private citizen to sell his home to an individual contrary to the wishes of the owner.

In California we witnessed a state Supreme Court taking under advisement the question as to whether or not it will compel a bank to make a loan to an applicant on the basis of his race. . . .

A Power-Hungry Government

The Supreme Court decisions have sanctioned enactment of the civil rights bill.

What this bill actually does is to empower the United States government to reallocate the entire productive capacity of the agricultural economy covered by quotas and acreage allotments of various types on the basis of race, creed, color and national origin.

It, in effect, places in the hands of the Federal government the right of a farmer to earn a living, making that right dependent upon the consent of the Federal government precisely as is the case in Russia.

The power is there. I am not in the least impressed by the protestations that the government will use this power with benevolent discretion.

We know that this bill authorizes the President of the United States to allocate all defense productive capacity of this country on the basis of race, creed, or color.

It does not matter in the least that he will make such allocations with restraint. The fact is that it is possible with a politically dominated agency to punish and to bankrupt and destroy any business that deals with the Federal government if it does not bow to the wishes and demands of the president of the United States.

All of us know what the court has done to capture the minds of our children.

The Federal judiciary has asserted the authority to prescribe regulations with respect to the management, operation, and control of our local schools. The second Brown decision [*Brown v. Board of Education* of Topeka, Kansas] in the infamous school

The 1964 Civil Rights Act gave greater political power to African Americans. Here, a woman votes in the 1964 presidential election.

segregation case authorized Federal district courts to supervise such matters as teacher hiring, firing, promotion, the expenditure of local funds, both administratively and for capital improvements, additions, and renovations, the location of new schools, the drawing of school boundaries, busing and transportation of school children, and, believe it or not, it has asserted the right in the Federal judiciary to pass judgment upon the curricula adopted in local public schools. . . .

In ruling after ruling, the Supreme Court has overstepped its constitutional authority. While appearing to protect the people's interest, it has in reality become a judicial tyrant.

It's the old pattern. The people always have some champion whom they set over them . . . and nurse into greatness. This, and no other, is the foot from which a tyrant springs, after first appearing as a protector.

This is another way of saying that the people never give up their liberties . . . and their freedom . . . but under some delusion.

But yet there is hope.

Take the Fight to the People

There is yet a spirit of resistance in this country which will not be oppressed. And it is awakening. And I am sure there is an abundance of good sense in this country which cannot be deceived.

I have personal knowledge of this. Thirty-four percent of the Wisconsin Democrats supported the beliefs you and I uphold and expound.

Thirty percent of the Democrats in Indiana join us in fighting this grab for executive power by those now in control in Washington.

And, listen to this, forty-three percent of the Democrats in Maryland, practically in view of the nation's capital, believe as you and I believe.

So, let me say to you today. Take heart. Millions of Americans believe just as we in this great region of the United States believe. . . .

Being a Southerner is no longer geographic. It's a philosophy and an attitude.

One destined to be a national philosophy—embraced by millions of Americans—which shall assume the mantle of leadership and steady a governmental structure in these days of crises.

Certainly I am a candidate for President of the United States.

If the left-wingers do not think I am serious—let them consider this.

I am going to take our fight to the people—the court of public opinion—where truth and common sense will eventually prevail. . . .

Conservatives of this nation constitute the balance of power in presidential elections.

I am a conservative.

I intend to give the American people a clear choice. I welcome a fight between our philosophy and the liberal left-wing dogma which now threatens to engulf every man, woman, and child in the United States.

I am in this race because I believe the American people have been pushed around long enough and that they, like you and I, are fed up with the continuing trend toward a socialist state which now subjects the individual to the dictates of an all-powerful central government.

I am running for President because I was born free. I want to remain free. I want your children and mine and our prosperity to be unencumbered by the manipulations of a soulless state.

I intend to fight for a positive, affirmative program to restore constitutional government and to stop the senseless bloodletting now being performed on the body of liberty by those who lead us willingly and dangerously close to a totalitarian central government.

In our nation, man has always been sovereign and the state has been his servant. This philosophy has made the United States the greatest free nation in history.

This freedom was not a gift. It was won by work, by sweat, by tears, by war, by whatever it took to be—and to remain free.

Are we today less resolute, less determined and courageous than our fathers and our grandfathers?

Are we to abandon this priceless heritage that has carried us to our present position of achievement and leadership?

I say if we are to abandon our heritage, let it be done in the open and full knowledge of what we do.

We are not unmindful and careless of our future. We will not stand aside while our conscientious convictions tell us that a dictatorial Supreme Court has taken away our rights and our liberties.

We will not stand idly by while the Supreme Court continues to invade the prerogatives left rightfully to the states by the constitution.

We must not be misled by left-wing incompetent news media that day after day feed us a diet of fantasy telling us we are bigots, racists and hate-mongers to oppose the destruction of the constitution and our nation.

A left-wing monster has risen up in this nation. It has invaded the government. It has invaded the news media. It has invaded the leadership of many of our churches. It has invaded every phase and aspect of the life of freedom-loving people. . . .

Politically evil men have combined and arranged themselves against us. The good people of this nation must now associate themselves together, else we will fall one by one, an unpitied sacrifice in a struggle which threatens to engulf the entire nation.

We can win. We can control the election of the President in November.

Our object must be our country, our whole country and nothing but our country.

If we will stand together—the people of this state—the people of my state—the people throughout this great region—yes, throughout the United States—then we can be the balance of power. We can determine who will be the next president. . . .

We are not going to change anything by sitting on our hands hoping that things will change for the better. Those who cherish individual freedom have a job to do.

First, let us let it be known that we intend to take the offensive and carry our fight for freedom across this nation. We will wield the power that is ours—the power of the people.

Let it be known that we will no longer tolerate the boot of tyranny. We will no longer hide our heads in the sand. We will re-school our thoughts in the lessons our forefathers knew so well.

We must destroy the power to dictate, to forbid, to require, to demand, to distribute, to edict, and to judge what is best and enforce that will of judgment upon free citizens.

We must revitalize a government founded in this nation on faith in god.

I ask that you join with me and that together, we give an active and courageous leadership to the millions of people throughout this nation who look with hope and faith to our fight to preserve our constitutional system of government with its guarantees of liberty and justice for all within the framework of our priceless freedoms.

The Harlem Riot of 1964

By Paul L. Montgomery

The Harlem Riot of 1964 began as a peaceful demonstration sponsored by CORE, the Congress of Racial Equality. Originally planned to protest the killing of three civil rights workers in Mississippi, the focus of the event changed when James Powell, a fifteen-year-old African American, was shot to death by a white police officer. The first two days of the demonstration were conducted without incident but mayhem broke out on the third day. Violence began at 9:30 P.M. on July 18, 1964, outside the 123rd police precinct.

Demonstrators, who were angered by police brutality in the death of Powell and filled with fury from years of white oppression, clashed with police. They threw bricks, looted stores, and lit garbage cans on fire. Rioting and looting continued for two nights before spreading to Brooklyn's Bedford-Stuyvesant neighborhood. The riot lasted for five days. Later, at the funeral for Powell, violence broke out again. In all, one person was killed and more than one hundred were injured with more than five hundred arrested.

As the civil rights movement progressed, so did racial rioting. Although the Harlem Riot of 1964 was smaller than riots that were to occur later in the decade, it was a landmark urban rebellion that underscored the deep frustrations of the African American community. Those frustrations were not curbed by the passage of the Civil Rights Act of 1964 just sixteen days earlier, and were exacerbated by the July 16, 1964, nomination of Republican presidential candidate Barry Goldwater, who many viewed as a racist. Despite progress in the civil rights movement there was a palpable feeling of dissatisfaction, especially among young, poor African Americans who were impatient for change to positively impact their lives.

Just two days after the riot began, internationally respected journalist and author Paul L. Montgomery chronicles the violent and historic events of the riot's first night in the following article for the *New York Times*.

A few minutes before 7 o'clock Saturday night a young woman from the Congress of Racial Equality [CORE] set up a rickety blue cafe chair and a child's American flag on the southwest corner of 125th Street and Seventh Avenue.

A desultory crowd of a hundred gathered in the steaming early evening and the rally began.

There was impatience with the heat, and anger over the shooting of a 15-year-old Negro boy by an off-duty white police lieutenant in [Manhattan's mostly-white Upper East Side neighborhood of] Yorkville two days before. But the crowd was not unruly, nor was there any air of violence.

Seven hours later screaming mobs, numbering in the thousands, thrashed back and forth through the center of Harlem, breaking windows, looting smashed storefronts, menacing policemen, and threatening or assaulting the few white people in the area.

Thousands of other residents watched in awe from their tenement windows or from sheltered places on the streets. More than 400 policemen who had sped to the scene fired thousands of shots in the air in an effort to control the crowds. Many who resisted police attempts to disperse the mobs were clubbed until they ran, or could no longer run.

At 123d Street and Seventh Avenue a jeering crowd of 600, several with bloodied heads, faced a grim group of white-helmeted troops from the Tactical Patrol Force. Bottles and garbage cans and garbage smashed around the policemen.

They crouched and fired volley after volley into the air, aiming just above the roofs. The night became acrid with gun-smoke.

"Go home, go home," a sweating red-faced captain shouted through a bullhorn.

A scream came back from a man in the mob: "We are home, baby."

What happened between the CORE rally on Saturday night

and the grim dawn of Sunday morning?

The rally was sponsored by three militant CORE chapters—Downtown, East River and South Jamaica. Its purpose had originally been to protest events in Mississippi, but the theme shifted after Thursday morning, when Lieut. Thomas Gilligan shot and killed 15-year-old James Powell in an apartment house doorway on East 76th Street.

The police say that the boy who was taking a voluntary remedial reading course at the Robert F. Wagner Junior High School nearby, moved toward the lieutenant with a knife. Several Negro witnesses have disputed this story and say the killing was unprovoked.

On the Harlem street corner Saturday night, a dozen patrolmen lounged and watched from nearby stations as Judith Howell, a 17-year-old member of Bronx CORE, spoke to the crowd from the blue chair. "James Powell was shot because he was black," the girl said. The crowd murmured assent and applauded. "We got a civil rights bill," she went on, "and along with the bill we got Barry Goldwater and a dead black boy."

The shifting crowd had grown to about 200. Several of them heckled the CORE speakers who followed.

"White people dictate your policy," one man yelled.

Chris Sprowal, chairman of Downtown CORE, said: "It is time to let 'the man' [white people] know that if he does something to us we are going to do something back. If you say 'You kick me once, I'm going to kick you twice,' we might get some respect."

Charles Saunders of South Jamaica CORE followed with the charge that "45 per cent of the cops in New York are neurotic murderers."

The crowd grew more excited, but not unruly. Then CORE turned the blue chair over to speakers in the crowd.

At about 8 P.M. the Rev. Nelson C. Dukes of the Fountain Springs Baptist Church, 15 West 126th Street, mounted the makeshift podium and gave a 20-minute speech.

Declaring it was time to stop talking and to act, he shouted that the people at the rally should march on the police station and present their demands. The crowd became more animated. There were shouts of "Let's go" and "Let's do it now."

A scar-faced man wearing a white sports shirt followed the preacher. His message was similar. "We have got to act now," he said.

Crowd Follows Silently

The meeting broke up at 8:35 P.M. "Let's go to the precinct," Mr. Dukes and the other man shouted. About a hundred spectators and CORE people followed them down Seventh Avenue to 123d Street, walking silently on the sidewalk.

They turned right at 123d Street, moving toward the 28th Precinct station house, halfway up the block on the uptown side. There they tried to force their way in, but were turned back and herded across the street by a squad of policemen.

A few bottles and garbage-can covers sailed toward the police. The policemen donned helmets and faced the crowd.

The crowd began taunting the policemen as some patrolmen rushed to the rooftops to stop the bottle-throwing.

"Murphy must be removed," they shouted, "Killers, murderers, Murphy's rats."

The patrolmen did not move. The precinct captain was asked how many men he had out. "Enough," he replied. There were about 20.

Demand That Murphy Act

Meanwhile Mr. Dukes, Ernest Russell of East River CORE, and a group of hangers-on presented their demands to Inspector Thomas V. Prendergast, who was in charge. They said they wanted Commissioner Murphy to come to Harlem and announce the suspension of Lieutenant Gilligan. They said they would not move until he did so.

At about 9:20—just at dusk—a truck carrying police barricades pulled up. As the barricades were being set up between the crowd and the police a scuffle broke out. It was the first violence of the long night.

About 25 patrolmen and demonstrators went down in a welter of flailing arms and legs.

"That's it," said Inspector Prendergast "Lock them up." The crowd by this time had grown to several hundred.

Sixteen demonstrators—including two CORE speakers from the rally—sat down on the sidewalk. All were rushed roughly across the street and into the station. Those from CORE took the characteristic nonviolent position of demonstrators—arms over the ears, knees tucked up to the chest. Others, who had not had training, were dragged into the station.

The crowd began shouting. The rain of bottles and debris increased. Dozens of policemen poured out of the station, buckling on holsters as they ran. One was struck on the head by a bottle and was sent to the hospital.

The force began pushing the crowd toward the Seventh and Eighth avenue ends of 123d Street amid a rain of bottles. A bus rolled up, and 48 members of the Tactical Patrol Force—the police shock troops—scrambled out.

Mr. Dukes looked on, shaking his head. "This has got out of hand," he said. "If I knew this was going to happen, I wouldn't have said anything." Then he walked away.

The fresh police forces established barricades on Seventh and Eighth avenues and cleared 123d Street between them. An emergency truck with a searchlight blocked the Seventh Avenue and was surrounded by white-helmeted policemen.

A crowd of 500 had formed by the searchlight and was constantly growing. Groups of youths stopped cars on Seventh Avenue on the downtown side. They picked out a car with a white couple in it and began pounding on it with their fists. One older man came up and broke a headlight with a bottle. The car finally got free of the 15 people surrounding it and careened away.

It was a little after 10 o'clock and Deputy Chief Inspector Harry Taylor had assumed command. Off-duty policemen, detectives and forces from other precincts began arriving. Between the barricades, 123d Street was clogged with police vehicles.

At Seventh Avenue, it was determined to break up the mob. Two squads of the Tactical Patrol Force, brandishing nightsticks and shouting "Charge!" leaped over the barricade and into the crowd.

In a turmoil, the mob broke into sections that eddied and flowed on Seventh Avenue between 122d and 124th Streets.

The first shots were fired at 10:30, at 125th Street and Lenox Avenue. A youth hurled a bottle of flaming gasoline at a squad car, and a sheet of flame spread on the street. A patrolman was burned, and his four companions emptied their revolvers into the night air.

The shots sounded like strings of firecrackers, except that there were flashes from the pistols. It was a sound that was to become familiar the rest of the night.

From 11 to midnight there was a lull in the area on Seventh Avenue, and it seemed that a near-riot had ended. Actually, five blocks away to the northeast, other groups on Lenox Avenue were breaking store windows and pillaging goods.

Reality—and Rumor

A drunken woman lay down on the northbound side of Seventh Avenue at 125th Street. Staring at the sky through an alcoholic haze, she said she just felt like lying down.

"They walk all over me in Greenville, S.C.," she said. "They might as well run over me here."

The crowd of several hundred on the corners attached a different interpretation to the scene. "Did you see that?" a man asked his companion. "They shot that woman down in cold blood." He glared at the handful of patrolmen near the resting woman.

"Women and children, beating up women and children," another remarked. A stout woman in a blue knit suit shouted to her group: "They are trying to pick us off one by one."

Just after midnight a tremendous volley of shots sounded from the northeast corner of 125th Street and Seventh Avenue. A dozen patrol cars, sirens screaming, raced down 125th Street to Lenox Avenue to answer an "assist patrolman" call.

Hundreds of people poured down 125th Street following the sirens. They raced along, shouting wildly as rock 'n' roll music floated down from a third-story dance hall. Older people, puffing and mopping their brows, trotted along to keep up.

The corner of 125th Street and Lenox Avenue was a disaster area. The ground was littered with broken glass and debris. Screaming crowds occupied each corner, pushing toward a ring of police cars and patrolmen crouched behind them. The police fired volley after volley into the air and over roofs as the crowd raced wildly back and forth.

Police reinforcements arrived at 125th and Lenox, and patrolmen began charging into the mobs on the corners. Some policemen had apparently reached the end of their patience. Anyone who did not move immediately when charged was set upon and clubbed.

Injured Removed

Shuttles of squad cars took away youths holding their heads. There were smears of blood up and down the sidewalks. These scenes were repeated up Lenox Avenue to 135th Street.

Screens protecting the windows of stores were ripped off and the stores looted. Every rifle in two pawnshops on 125th Street was gone. Grocery stores, and insurance agency, a men's clothing store and many others were sacked.

Volleys of shots rang up and down the avenue and the spent cartridges littered the pavement.

A woman who had been struck by a hit-and-run driver lay on 125th Street, surrounded by friends and policemen. The rain of bottles continued and the crowds shouted, "Murderers!" at the police.

About 2 A.M. the main thrust of the riot seemed to have been spent, although there were sporadic incidents until dawn.

The 28th Precinct communications were snarled by the avalanche of calls. False alarms were frequent and fire equipment raced here and there.

Sometime after 4 a figure stumbled through the police barricade at 123d and Seventh Avenue and went toward the precinct house. He was a white youth with a bloody mouth and glazed eyes. He sobbed uncontrollably. Through numb lips he told the police that he was a sailor who had got off at the wrong subway stop.

He had been set upon by a group of youths, he said. "They beat me. They beat me and took my watch and I yelled. I'm a sailor from California, and I took the wrong subway train."

As dawn broke near 6 the squads of patrolmen, many of whom had been working for 14 hours, began filing back to the station.

Travels with the Merry Pranksters

By Paul Perry

In the summer of 1964, author Ken Kesey and a group of thirteen friends climbed into a remodeled school bus painted in Day-Glo colors with psychedelic designs. They named the bus FURTHUR, a fusion of the words "further" and "future" and used it to travel around the country in the summer of 1964. They began in La Honda, California, traveled counterclockwise around the fringes of the nation, and ended up in Big Sur, California. Their trip, which is chronicled by author Paul Perry in his 1990 book *On the Bus*, was a seminal event in the birth of the sixties counterculture. The counterculture embraced a bohemian lifestyle and rejected the cultural mores of the day.

The friends called themselves the "Merry Pranksters" and included such counterculture icons as Timothy Leary and Neal Cassady. Riding on the success of his debut novel *One Flew over the Cuckoo's Nest*, Kesey financed most of the trip out of his own pocket. He and his friends recorded the events of the trip on film and tape with hopes of a future theatrical release, but attempts to create a cogent work from the miles of film footage ultimately failed.

Kesey and the Merry Pranksters traveled from San Francisco to New York in part so that Kesey could promote his new novel *Sometimes a Great Notion*. The trip itself, however, made the more indelible impact on American culture when it was sensationalized in Tom Wolfe's 1967 book *The Electric Kool-Aid Acid Test*. It continues to influence new generations. The impact of Kesey and the Merry Pranksters can be seen not only in the literature of the 60s but also in films such as 1969's *Easy Rider* and the long-popular music of the Grateful Dead.

T he bus trip began on June 14, 1964.
There were so many different agendas going into the bus trip that it's almost impossible to say exactly what it was *supposed* to be. The reality is that it became a metaphor for the carefree (and, at times, careless), hedonistic, authority-challenging, back-to-nature, alternative-seeking qualities of the 1960s. If there was one thing that Kesey and the Pranksters stood for, it was the power of individuals to stand up and be themselves, for each person to "be as big as he feels it's in him to be."

Twenty-five years after the bus trip, Kesey described its purpose to *Stanford Magazine* in terms no less grand than these: "What we hoped was that we could stop the coming end of the world."

In the unique fashion of the 1960s, the Pranksters' utopian idealism was almost always mixed with logic-eluding nonsense. Of course, this nonsense had its own purpose: When rationality is the tool of authority being irrational is a way to be free. It's also a way to avoid the rational expectations that inhibit spontaneity and creativity.

Kesey demonstrated this kind of thinking in an interview with Pacifica Radio in San Francisco in 1967, when he was asked to define what the Pranksters were doing.

> *Kesey*: As navigator of this venture I try as much as possible to set out in a direction that, in the first place, is practically impossible to achieve, and then, along the way, mess up the minds of the crew with as many chemicals as we can lay our hands on, so it's almost certain that we can't get there.
>
> *Question*: Well, would you say that it was deliberately self-defeating, then?
>
> *Kesey*: This is about as deliberately self-defeating as anything has ever been in history. Most of the people, I think, involved in this realize that there's nothing to be gained.

This philosophy is a reflection of the methods Kesey brought to his own literary work. After *Cuckoo's Nest* was completed, he returned to Oregon where he worked as a logger to gather material for *Sometimes a Great Notion*. His approach to *Notion* was

somewhat free-form, the way a jazz musician might start an in-
teresting riff without necessarily knowing where he'll go with it.
As he told an interviewer at a Palo Alto newspaper:

> In *Cuckoo's Nest* I had the answer before I started. But with this
> latest book I didn't have the answer. Therefore, it was a good
> deal more painful, and cost a lot more sweat. I was struggling
> with myself as to whether I should continue on or quit. When I
> speak of quitting, I mean both living and writing. I contemplated
> suicide—only in the manner in which I toyed with insanity while
> writing the other book. But there are many forms of suicide.

The story itself is about a strong-minded family of loggers
who decide to buck union strikers and keep logging. But the
techniques Kesey used are experimental, in the masterful tradition of the works of a James Joyce or William Faulkner. Tenses
change in mid-paragraph, as do points of view; yet these shifting perspectives (acid-inspired?) make for a more complete picture of the blustery world of the Stamper family. Using these
techniques and weaving a story that didn't have a preconceived
story line was a gigantic task, but the result was a book that some
have called a masterpiece. As he told a Bay Area newspaper:

> The book was difficult because its technique was completely
> new. I had no way of knowing when I was writing whether I was
> making any contact or not.

"I don't think I'll ever be able to do that again," Kesey recently
told *Stanford Magazine*, referring to this method of writing.

After living the life of a literary monk, Kesey's agenda for the
bus trip may have been partially to get some much-needed rest
and relaxation. It may also have been to gather material for another book, or to pursue another medium, as many of his Stanford [University] friends declared, and as the cameras and sound
equipment hinted. Or maybe it was just to go see the [1964 New
York] World's Fair and attend his publication party for *Sometimes a Great Notion*. Whatever his reasons, he wasn't the only
person directing the voyage.

Many of the other "Pranksters" took the trip just to get to the
East. Jane ("Generally Famished") Burton, who was a neighbor
of Kesey's and a member of the old Perry Lane gang, and Steve
("Zonker") Lambrecht were going to see friends in New York
City. Paula ("Gretchen Fetchin") Sundsten was on her way to a

waitressing job at a restaurant owned by the former boxer Jack Dempsey. Both Gretchen and Zonker eventually stayed with the bus and returned to California.

Some of the Pranksters believed they were producing art from the beginning of the trip—*spontaneous* art of the let-it-happen-and-see-what-develops-on-the-film school of artistic expression. These were the hardcore Pranksters, who included Ken ("The Intrepid Traveller") Babbs, who had just gotten out of the Marine Corps after a stint as a helicopter pilot in Vietnam; Sandy ("Dismount") Lehmann-Haupt; George ("Hardly Visible") Walker; Mike ("Mal Function") Hagen, a frat brother of Kesey's from the University of Oregon; Ron ("Hassler") Bevirt who, fresh from a tour of duty in the Army, was along to try his hand at still photography; and Kathy Casano, who later earned the name "Stark Naked," came along because Hagen offered to make her a movie star. They believed in the trip's artistic possibilities. Also on board were Ken's brother Chuck ("Brother Charlie") and his cousin Dale ("Highly Charged") Kesey, along with Babbs's brother John ("Sometimes Missing"), who were basically on the bus to tour the country and ride with friends.

And then, of course, there was Neal Cassady ("Sir Speed Limit"), who came along just a few days before the trip started. He approached the task of driving as a professional, but it was a job he was uniquely suited for and he no doubt enjoyed it. He was an instinctual driver with the uncanny ability to stay up almost continuously and talk constantly while he did it.

All told, there were fourteen people on the bus who became known as the Merry Band of Pranksters. They spent $70,000 (most of it Kesey's money from book advances and movie rights) buying gasoline, road food ("ratburgers," according to Ken Babbs), and miles and miles of 16-millimeter film and audio-tape. Approximately fifty hours of film and hundreds of hours of audio-tape recorded virtually every dramatic encounter, babble, moan, and road sign of this immortal trip. The purpose of all this documentation was to make a movie, *The Merry Pranksters Search for the Cool Place.*

What has come of it, since the trip 25 years ago, is a still-massive work-in-progress. Despite weeks, months, some say *years* of attempts to make sense of it all by Kesey, Ken Babbs, and others (including Hollywood producers), *The Merry Pranksters Search for the Cool Place* hasn't yet been edited into a theatrical release, though parts of it have appeared in the lectures-shows given by Ken Babbs, who speculates that its future may lie in video.

Of course, no one knew these things at the time. They simply did the best they could to record the scenes of the trip: Neal Cassady driving the bus across Texas, the camera trained on his handsome face as he smoked a joint, made faces, and rapped continuously—*all at the same time*! Kesey on top of the bus in Alabama, playing the flute with an American flag wrapped around his head like Captain America. Gretch buying ratburgers in the Deep South. Babbs "performing surgery" with gin and tampons on a festering bug bite on Hagen's leg. And the whole bunch of them welcoming a teenaged runaway on board, who strips to her skivvies as the Pranksters paint her nubile body the colors of the magic bus.

They *filmed, filmed, filmed* all across America, nine stops in all: from California through Arizona; through Texas; through Louisiana; through parts of Florida, before making a left turn and heading up to New York to see Cassady's old buddy Jack Kerouac and the media's LSD gurus Timothy Leary and Richard Alpert. They did finally attend the New York World's Fair.

With this film the Pranksters set about, as one of their tribal songs went, to "change the course of time"—and perhaps someday earn some pranking capital.

As the Pranksters' legend grew, this cross-country voyage gained a mythical status. But as in other myths—Homer's *Odyssey*, or, closer to home, Kerouac's *On the Road*—it's easy to overlook that the voyage itself was a string of days and nights of grinding intercontinental travel in an antiquated bus.

"You have to realize," says Ron Bevirt, "that this was an unpleasant trip. It was noisy and chaotic on the bus. Some people wanted to be left alone and others wanted to keep sticking a camera in everyone's face. On top of that, it was hot. This was summer and we were going through the South. We couldn't get cool. We couldn't stop sweating. At times we couldn't hear anything but the noise of the bus. [But] the most memorable experiences are often the most unpleasant ones."

It was only later that people realized that the bus trip was the beginning of a cultural myth. From the trip came the slogan "You're either on the bus or off the bus." Implying, of course, that it's hip to be "on." But no one knew at the time exactly how hip it might someday seem to have been on the bus.

Mississippi— "Everybody's Scared"

By *Newsweek*

Thousands of civil rights activists, many of them idealistic college students, headed to Mississippi during the summer of 1964. At the time, Mississippi was a bastion of black poverty with a disgraceful voting rights record. The activists' goal was to join with local African American citizens to expand black voter registration, teach reading and math to black children, and aid indigent blacks in obtaining legal and medical assistance.

The Freedom Summer campaign was organized by a coalition of groups led by the Congress of Racial Equality (CORE) and including the National Association for the Advancement of Colored People (NAACP) and the Student Nonviolent Coordinating Committee (SNCC). The formation of the Mississippi Freedom Democratic Party (MFDP) was a major focus of the summer program. The new party elected a slate of sixty-eight delegates to the national Democratic Party convention. Although they failed to unseat the delegates representing the state's all-white Democratic Party, they did draw national attention to the issue of race discrimination. The groups also established thirty "Freedom Schools" to improve education for blacks throughout the state, which became a model for programs like Head Start.

Freedom Summer activists were threatened and harassed throughout their travels in Mississippi. Freedom school buildings and volunteers' homes were often targeted. Also, thirty-seven black churches, and thirty black homes and businesses were firebombed or burned that summer.

But the most infamous act of violence was the murder of three young
civil rights workers. James Chaney, a black volunteer, and two white
activists, Andrew Goodman and Michael Schwerner were last seen
alive on June 21, 1964. Their bodies were discovered six weeks later:
Chaney had been savagely beaten, while Goodman and Schwerner had
died of gunshot wounds. The murders made headlines, provoked national outrage, and generated increased support for the civil rights
movement. The following article from *Newsweek* magazine details the
events surrounding the disappearance of those three young men.

T hey were three in the first wave riding south into another
country, full of dreams that they could change it with
words and books and young ideals, full of fear that they
might never leave it alive. They struck camp in Ohio one damp
morning before dawn and rode down in a day, nibbling pretzels
and potato chips, gazing out at the bluegrass and the rolling red
hills and the dusty cotton fields, talking about what it would be
like in Mississippi. By dusk, they arrived in Meridian. And the
next day they were gone.

Thus, the very day it began last week, the "freedom summer"
campaign mounted by a coalition of civil-rights groups in the
most rigidly segregated state in the U.S. escalated into a crisis of
national dimensions. To white Mississippi, the 175 Northern students who arrived last week—and the 800 more still to come—
seemed an invading army bent on destroying its way of life. And
white Mississippi was afraid. A spate of intimidation—bombings, church burnings, harassment arrests—began even before
the advance guard arrived. And then the three young men—two
white New Yorkers and a black Mississippian—simply disap-
peared into 24 square miles of swamp and scrub pine and scrag-
gly cotton land known as Neshoba County, with no trace but the
burned-out shell of their car. Officially, at the weekend, they were
missing; unofficially, few doubted that they were the first mar-
tyrs of a fiery Mississippi summer.

Would they be only the first? The question posed a grave
dilemma for the Federal government. Lyndon B. Johnson quickly
established a Federal presence in the state—first, FBI reinforcements, then ex-CIA director Allen Dulles, finally 100 sailors to
help in the search. Plainly, he hoped that would be enough. But
he was under heavy pressure to take the next step—dispatching

U.S. marshals or even troops to Mississippi to protect the students if local lawmen would not or could not. And there were those in Washington who feared that the summer so grimly begun might yet end in a Federal occupation amounting to no less than a second Reconstruction.

Amateurs

That was precisely what some Negro leaders hoped for. With few new Negro voters to show after years of registration campaigning by the civil-rights professionals, the leaders mustered student amateurs as a means of involving the nation in their drive. They knew the peril; the likelihood of violence was lecture Topic A for the volunteers at their training camp at Western College for Women in Oxford, Ohio.

Fear rode south from Oxford with Michael Schwerner, Andrew Goodman, James Chaney, and five fellow volunteers that damp Saturday morning. Six months before, Schwerner, a stocky, goateed social worker of 24, had quit his job at a settlement house on Manhattan's Lower East Side to work full-time for the Congress of Racial Equality. CORE sent him and his wife, Rita, 22, to set up a community center in a shabby office suite over Fielder's Drugstore in Meridian—the first of a dozen such centers planned for the summer.

Among their first recruits was Jim Chaney, 21, a bright, elfin Meridian Negro who had quit school in the eleventh grade to work as a plasterer's apprentice. "Mama," he told his mother the day he joined the Schwerners, "I believe I done found an organization that I can be in and do something for myself and somebody else, too."

"Ain't you afraid of this?"

"Naw, mama, that's what's the matter now—everybody's scared."

He went to work full-time, helping fit the center with a sewing machine, a Ping Pong table, and a 1,000-book library, riding church to church with the Schwerners to coax the frightened Negroes to come to the center. "At first, most were afraid," Rita Schwerner said. "But, by the first week, we had seven kids at a story-reading hour, and from there things just kind of grew."

"Always Phone"

Goodman, a 20-year-old Queens College anthropology major, was assigned to their task force at Oxford and joined them on the ride south in a CORE station wagon. At Chaney's suggestion, they set out at 3:30 A.M. to avoid reaching Meridian after dark. Again and again, on the way, Schwerner hammered at a single point: "Always phone in to let everybody know where you are if you leave the office." Goodman and the five other students listened and gazed at the alien landscape and thought about their private fears.

Next morning, the three drew their first assignment: investigating the burning of a Negro church at Longdale, in neighboring Neshoba County. Schwerner picked up the file at the Meridian office—it was under "I" for "Intimidation"—and told a co-worker: "If we aren't back by 4, you start calling."

They weren't. They drove to Longdale, questioned Negroes about the burning, poked around in the charred rubble of Mount Zion Methodist Church, then set out for the county seat, Philadelphia, 12 miles away. On the outskirts of town, Deputy Sheriff Cecil Price, 26, stopped their station wagon, arrested Chaney for speeding and the others for "investigation," and took them to jail—where all three were logged in at first as "Negro males."

Niceties

At 10:30 P.M.—five hours later—Chaney paid a $20 traffic fine and they were freed. "They were just as nice as could be, and I was nice to them," Price said blandly. "I told them to leave the county, but not the U.S." By Price's account, a patrol car tailed them for a few blocks and saw them off down Highway 19 toward Meridian, 39 miles southeast. Then they vanished.

White Mississippi tried hard to believe that it was a hoax. "If they are missing," growled barrel-chested Sheriff L.A. Rainey, "they're just hiding out somewhere and trying to cause us a lot of trouble somehow." But two days later, on a tip, FBI agents found the fire-gutted station wagon ditched in a thicket of blackberry and sweetgum at the edge of Bogue Chitto Swamp—15 miles *northeast* of Philadelphia. There were no bullet holes, no bloodstains—and no sign of the missing three.

Reaction was swift. FBI director J. Edgar Hoover telephoned word of the discovery to President Johnson just as the parents of the two missing New Yorkers arrived at his office to plead for Federal intervention. Mr. Johnson could only break the disquieting news to them and assure them that the government was doing all it could.

Sympathy

How much could it do? Civil-rights leaders wanted U.S. marshals to guard the students; so did the parents of those already in the state and those still to come. Convening in Washington when the news arrived, some 2,000 NAACP convention delegates marched on the Justice Department and sent executive secretary Roy Wilkins to ask Attorney General Robert F. Kennedy for "preventive action rather than ambulatory action such as picking up the bodies afterward." Kennedy was sympathetic; he went outside after the meeting to watch the demonstration with the widow of an earlier Mississippi martyr, Medgar Evers, and to shake hands with some of the pickets. But, as he told Wilkins, the government's constitutional power to move in was questionable at best. More than that, granted even the authority and the will to use it, civil-rights workers traveling the dusty, dangerous Mississippi back country could scarcely be tendered protection short of a full-scale Federal occupation of the state.

Instead, the government strategy was to intervene just enough—so the hope ran—to pressure Mississippi to keep the peace on its own. The President kept up a running telephone dialogue with Gov. Paul B. Johnson Jr. He rushed out-of-state FBI agents to Philadelphia. He sent in a crew of unarmed, fatigue-clad sailors from nearby Meridian Naval Air Station to join the search through the hardscrabble Neshoba farm country and snake-infested swamp. And he dispatched Allen Dulles to Mississippi for an avuncular two-day round of talks with the governor, state officials, and civil-rights leaders. Dulles came home with a firm recommendation for stepped-up FBI action to "control and prosecute terroristic activity" in cooperation with Mississippi authorities—and more Federal measures "as appropriate" to keep the peace. And Mr. Johnson agreed to augment the FBI force.

Orthodoxy

Slow to move at first, the governor did order state troopers into the search—and, at the weekend, went to Philadelphia himself to appeal to county residents to pitch in. As he had all along, he catered to the orthodox view that Negro "extremists" were to blame for Mississippi's troubles and that the missing three might really be in hiding ("They could be in Cuba . . . I would be a very large fool if I made a guess"). But Johnson, a law-and-order segregationist, was worried enough to keep looking. "It may not be in my lifetime," he said, "but they'll be found."

For both Johnsons—the President and the governor—a central fact remained: Mississippi's summer could not be wished away. If their very presence was a provocation, the students were in Mississippi by constitutional right, for ends to which the government is itself committed; the governor could not wall them out—nor could the President, even if he were so inclined, ask them to pull out. And the students themselves were in no mood to turn back, despite the disappearance of their fellow soldiers and the burnings and the bombings that punctuated the week. Leaders relayed the news to them and told them it would be no disgrace to leave. But at the weekend, a fresh wave moved into Mississippi.

The Lie That Launched Vietnam: The Tonkin Gulf Incident

Part I by Lyndon B. Johnson; Part II by Tom Wells

The official story was that North Vietnamese torpedo boats launched an unprovoked attack against a U.S. destroyer that was on a routine patrol in the Vietnamese Gulf of Tonkin on August 2, 1964. Two days later the Pentagon announced that a second attack by North Vietnamese PT boats had occurred earlier in the day. That evening President Lyndon B. Johnson went on national television to tell the American people about this critical escalation of conflict in Southeast Asia. Editorial writers around the country commended the president for his candor. The *Los Angeles Times* urged Americans to "face the fact that the Communists, by their attack on American vessels in international waters, have themselves escalated the hostilities."

Johnson's television address resulted in the passage of the Tonkin Gulf Resolution, in essence a declaration of war against North Vietnam. The August 7, 1964, resolution authorized the president "to take all necessary measures to repel any armed attack against the forces of the United States and to prevent further aggression." Only two senators, Wayne Morse of Oregon and Ernest Gruening of Alaska, voted against the resolution, which was carried unanimously in the House of

Part I: Lyndon B. Johnson, televised address, August 4, 1964. Part II: Tom Wells, *The War Within: America's Battle over Vietnam*. Berkeley, CA: University of California Press, 1994. Copyright © 1994 by the Regents of the University of California. Reproduced by permission of the author.

Representatives. Congress later grew to regret passage of the resolution, repealing it in 1971.

The truth of the Tonkin Gulf incident was markedly different from what the president disclosed to the public on the evening of August 4, 1964. In his book *The War Within: America's Battle over Vietnam*, sociologist Tom Wells describes the events at the Gulf of Tonkin, starting with Operation 34-A, a military offensive against the North Vietnamese begun earlier in the year and directed by Defense Secretary Robert McNamara. Operation 34-A included air attacks against North Vietnam, commando raids against North Vietnamese bridges, and patrols into North Vietnamese territorial waters, including the Gulf of Tonkin, in retaliation for North Vietnam's incursions into South Vietnam.

Not surprisingly, North Vietnamese officials in Hanoi refuted the U.S. account of events and, in fact, dissenting senator Morse questioned it as well after learning of amphibious raids on North Vietnamese that had occurred just days before the incident. McNamara denied any connection between the two events. Navy pilot and squadron commander James Stockdale who was a witness to the incident stated, "I had the best seat in the house to watch that event and our destroyers were just shooting at phantom targets—there were no PT boats out there. . . . There was nothing there but black water and American fire power."

The media, however, relayed the official version of the events. Their blind acceptance of the Johnson administration's reports fueled the fire of escalation and aided the passage of the Tonkin Resolution. The Vietnam War, a bloody conflict resulting in more than fifty thousand American deaths and millions of Vietnamese casualties, lasted until 1975 when the United States withdrew from the war and South Vietnam collapsed.

Part I of the following selection is the text from President Johnson's televised address to the nation. Part II is an excerpt from author Tom Wells's book *The War Within: America's Battle over Vietnam*. Combined, they give insight into both the official and historical views of the Tonkin Gulf incident.

I

My fellow Americans: As President and Commander in Chief, it is my duty to the American people to report that renewed hostile actions against United States ships on the high seas in the Gulf of Tonkin have today required me to order the military forces of the United States to take action in reply.

The initial attack on the destroyer *Maddox*, on August 2 [1964], was repeated today by a number of hostile vessels attacking two U.S. destroyers with torpedoes. The destroyers and supporting aircraft acted at once on the orders I gave after the initial act of aggression. We believe at least two of the attacking boats were sunk. There were no U.S. losses.

The performance of commanders and crews in this engagement is in the highest tradition of the United States Navy. But repeated acts of violence against the Armed Forces of the United States must be met not only with alert defense, but with positive reply. That reply is being given as I speak to you tonight. Air action is now in execution against gunboats and certain supporting facilities in North Vietnam which have been used in these hostile operations.

In the larger sense this new act of aggression, aimed directly at our own forces, again brings home to all of us in the United States the importance of the struggle for peace and security in Southeast Asia. Aggression by terror against the peaceful villagers of South Vietnam has now been joined by open aggression on the high seas against the United States of America.

No Wider War

The determination of all Americans to carry out our full commitment to the people and to the government of South Vietnam will be redoubled by this outrage. Yet our response, for the present, will be limited and fitting. We Americans know, although others appear to forget, the risks of spreading conflict. We still seek no wider war.

I have instructed the Secretary of State [Dean Rusk] to make this position totally clear to friends and to adversaries and, indeed, to all. I have instructed Ambassador [to the United Nations, Adlai] Stevenson to raise this matter immediately and urgently before the Security Council of the United Nations. Finally, I have today met with the leaders of both parties in the Congress of the United States and I have informed them that I shall immediately request the Congress to pass a resolution making it clear that our Government is united in its determination to take all necessary measures in support of freedom and in defense of peace in Southeast Asia.

I have been given encouraging assurance by these leaders of both parties that such a resolution will be promptly introduced, freely and expeditiously debated, and passed with overwhelming support. And just a few minutes ago I was able to reach Senator [Barry] Goldwater [Republican candidate for president] and I am glad to say that he has expressed his support of the statement that I am making to you tonight.

It is a solemn responsibility to have to order even limited military action by forces whose overall strength is as vast and as awesome as those of the United States of America, but it is my considered conviction, shared throughout your Government, that firmness in the right is indispensable today for peace; that firmness will always be measured. Its mission is peace.

II

Operation 34-A proceeded in earnest in the summer of 1964. Under the cover of night, squads of South Vietnamese saboteurs parachuted into North Vietnam to blow up bridges, railroads, munitions depots, waterworks. Propagandists rained leaflets from the sky and engineered radio broadcasts from ships offshore. South Vietnamese agents kidnapped citizens of North Vietnam to extract intelligence. American-made Swift boats manned by South Vietnamese commandos peppered North Vietnamese coastal and island installations with cannon and machine-gun fire.

According to Marshall Green, a senior U.S. State Department official at the time, Operation 34-A was "a fiasco. . . . A *terrible* disappointment. Nothing seemed to work." Despite receiving unbridled American support and guidance, the South Vietnamese obviously "had no capability to strike against the North, even in a subversive way like this." They "just didn't have the stuff." Jittery South Vietnamese paratroopers failed to report for their missions. Their officers periodically showed up in drunken stupors designed to render them unfit for service. Those guerrillas who did make it into North Vietnam would often "never show up again"; they were "like sitting ducks."

In Washington, one option took center stage. Bomb. Convinced that the mushrooming revolution in South Vietnam was manufactured in Hanoi, the Johnson administration prepared a plan for graduated air strikes against the North, culminating in sharp blows. The State Department's Walt Rostow, inspired by his experience picking bombing targets during World War II (Rostow

The Vietnam War resulted in the devastation of homes and entire villages. Here, women salvage belongings after a Vietcong attack.

knew bombing) and persuaded that peasant revolutions could be squelched by cutting off their external sources of support, joined the Joint Chiefs of Staff (JCS) in calling for decisive strikes.

Most administration principals were reluctant to move toward overt escalation, however. It might arouse China and the Soviet Union, they feared, and worry America's allies. It might also prompt the enemy to step up his attacks on the shaky Saigon government. Not least forbidding, it would probably evoke consternation at home; short months before the presidential election, this was a poor time to upset the public. Some politicking was necessary before asking the American people to join a crusade.

At a high-level strategy conference in June, securing a supportive congressional resolution "prior to wider U.S. action" was a key concern. Secretary of State Dean Rusk argued that public opinion on U.S. policy was "badly divided" and that President Johnson therefore required "an affirmation of support." Assistant Secretary of State for East Asian and Pacific Affairs William Bundy stressed the need for an "urgent" public relations campaign "to get at the basic doubts of the value of Southeast Asia and the importance of our stake there." With Johnson's apparent encouragement, the State Department began assembling information for answering "prevalent public questions" on the war. Officials dispensed a steady stream of leaks to the press professing America's intention to stand up to "aggression" in Vietnam.

The Events of the Incident

Then came the Tonkin Gulf incidents. In the early morning hours of July 31, 1964, four Swift boats under the direction of General William Westmoreland, commander of U.S. forces in Vietnam, attacked two small North Vietnamese islands. While the attacks were occurring, the U.S. destroyer *Maddox* was steaming menacingly toward the area. The next day, and again on August 2, T-28 bombers deposited their payloads on North Vietnamese villages near the Laotian border.

On the afternoon of August 2, the enemy struck back. Three North Vietnamese torpedo boats launched a high-speed run at the *Maddox*. One of the boats was knocked dead in the water by jets from a U.S. aircraft carrier nearby, and the others were disabled. Hours later President Johnson ordered the U.S. destroyer *C. Turner Joy* to join the *Maddox* in its muscular patrol of the gulf. "The other side got a sting out of this," Rusk told reporters. "If they do it again, they'll get another sting." That seemed to be the intention. On the night of August 3, the United States orchestrated two more Swift boat raids against North Vietnam. Both American destroyers had been informed of the raids in advance.

The next evening, the *Maddox*'s radar detected what appeared to be rapidly closing targets. Over twenty times, the ship's sonarman shouted "Torpedoes in the water," causing the *Maddox* and *Turner Joy* to cut erratically across the sea. Although the *Turner Joy* repeatedly reported the ranges of the targets at which it was firing, the *Maddox*'s radar could discern nothing since the first readings. The *Maddox* was, in fact, even having difficulty locating the *Turner Joy*.

Near midnight, the *Maddox*'s gun director was given a range reading of the "firmest target we've had all night." "It was a damned big one, right on us," he said later. "No doubt about this one." Just as he was about to squeeze the firing key, however, the gun director realized something was seriously wrong. "'Where is the *Turner Joy?*'" he shouted. "There was a lot of yelling of 'Goddamn' back and forth, with the bridge telling me to 'fire before we lose contact,' and me yelling right back at them," the gun director recalled. "I finally told them, 'I'm not opening fire until I know where the *Turner Joy* is'" The bridge directed the *Turner Joy* to turn on its lights "Sure enough, there she was, right in the cross hairs. I had six five-inch guns [aimed] right at the *Turner Joy*. . . . If I had fired, it would have blown it clean out of the water. In fact, I could have been shot for *not* squeezing the trigger."

At 11 A.M. Washington time, Navy authorities in the Pacific sent the Pentagon a FLASH message indicating the two destroyers were engaged in combat. Several hours later, President Johnson ordered Operation Pierce Arrow "reprisal" strikes against four North Vietnamese torpedo boat bases and an oil-storage depot. While rejecting pleas from the JCS to "clobber" Hanoi, he dispatched air assault forces to Southeast Asia capable of initiating a sustained bombing campaign against the North. He also decided to immediately seek a congressional resolution declaring war.

Late that afternoon, Admiral Ulysses S. Grant Sharp, commander in chief, Pacific (CINCPAC), conveyed some disquieting news to Secretary of Defense Robert McNamara. It was unclear to officers on the spot whether the two U.S. ships had actually been attacked. Before Sharp could get back to him with confirming evidence, McNamara gave the formal execute order for the reprisal strikes. It is now apparent that the attacks never took place. In early 1965, Johnson offered the episode as an example of "what I have to put up with" at the Pentagon. "For all I know, our Navy was shooting at whales out there," he said.

On August 7, Congress passed the Southeast Asia Resolution granting Johnson the considerable power to "take all necessary measures to repel any armed attacks against the forces of the United States and to prevent further aggression." Only two senators—Wayne Morse (D-Oreg.) and Ernest Gruening (D-Alas.)—voted against it. The House of Representatives was even more compliant: it passed the resolution unanimously.

Following the Gulf of Tonkin affair, Johnson's popularity in the Harris poll catapulted from 42 to 72 percent overnight; support for his Vietnam policies increased from 58 to 85 percent. Despite the opposition of Morse and Gruening, the questioning of a few other senators, and a handful of small peace demonstrations, the administration's domestic rear guard appeared safe after all.

The Free Speech Movement

By David Burner

The Free Speech Movement was born at the University of California at Berkeley in the fall of 1964, but its birth was not spontaneous. Pressure had been building for years beginning in the late 1950s when students began to form advocacy organizations devoted to controversial social issues. They took on causes such as nuclear testing, capital punishment, and civil rights. Student activism was growing on college campuses all across the country with UC Berkeley students at the forefront.

In 1960, students joined together to protest the San Francisco hearings of Senator Joseph McCarthy's House Un-American Activities Committee (HUAC). Conceived as a means of ferreting out individuals and organizations that posed a Communist threat to national security, HUAC's activities had evolved into a witch hunt that had disrupted lives and ruined the careers of those who were publicly labeled as "Reds." Students were upset by the committee's infringement on civil liberties and took action. Although many were arrested during the anti-HUAC protest, their efforts had an impact that ultimately helped lead to the dissolution of HUAC.

Empowered by their success, the students continued their activism. However, their increasingly public profile and sometimes radical liberal views began to anger conservatives and business leaders in the Berkeley community who called on university officials to curb students' noneducational activities. By fall of 1964 the situation came to a

David Burner, *Making Peace with the Sixties*. Princeton, NJ: Princeton University Press, 1996. Copyright © 1996 by Princeton University Press. Reproduced by permission.

head, dividing the community and threatening the very fabric of life at UC Berkeley.

Historian David Burner, a professor of history at the State University of New York at Stonybrook profiles the birth of the Free Speech Movement in his 1996 book *Making Peace with the Sixties.*

Between 1963 and 1964 the number of entering freshmen at the University of California at Berkeley increased by 37 percent. In the previous decade students majoring in the more socially conscious humanities and social sciences had jumped from 36 to 50 percent. Clark Kerr, president of the multicampus University of California system, had planned for the arrival of masses of new students. But he failed to see the attendant problems. He presided over an institution, committed to acting *in loco parentis*, that in this new time of student ferment and enormous growth could no longer do so. Academic conservatives complained that administrators and faculty members were no longer supervising their young charges' thought and behavior; students were soon complaining of the vestiges of that supervision.

Kerr, a liberal Quaker and a Democrat, had helped squelch a faculty loyalty oath imposed by the California legislature back in the McCarthy era. Yet he often compromised. In 1961, he refused to allow [controversial civil rights leader] Malcolm X to appear on campus; his grounds were that Malcolm was a sectarian religious leader. But he did not block the less controversial Billy Graham, the prominent evangelical preacher. On another occasion he kept Herbert Aptheker, editor of the American Communist party's theoretical journal, from speaking. In 1963 Kerr lifted a ban against communist speakers, but to get the university Regents' approval he instituted a yardstick he himself disliked: spokesmen for traditional views would have to follow controversial speakers. In all, he was a prototype of the liberal who would be caught in the conflicting demands of his time. That is likely a fair description of much of the administration at Berkeley. The maneuvers, at times ham-handed and at others conciliatory, of Berkeley officialdom in 1964 and 1965 attest to the dilemmas of liberals confronted by a radicalism that they had neither the wish to stifle nor the will to embrace. . . .

In September 1964 Mario Savio, the son of a Roman Catholic machinist proud of his son's commitment to social justice, returned to campus after teaching at a [Mississippi Freedom Summer] freedom school in McComb during that greatest of Mississippi summers. Savio discovered that the campus authorities had declared off limits for advocates of civil rights and other causes a stretch of Telegraph Avenue, the Bancroft strip, just outside the main gate to the Berkeley campus. For years the strip had been accepted as a place where students could hand out pamphlets, solicit names for petitions, and sign people up. But recently it had become identified with demonstrations against Berkeley and Oakland businesses that practiced discrimination. One of the demonstrators' chief targets was the *Oakland Tribune*, the East Bay newspaper published by William Knowland, the conservative United States Senator. The students' activities antagonized conservative university Regents and they pressured Berkeley to close the campus as a recruiting ground for activists and restrict student agitation in adjacent areas.

The ban set off a firestorm. Students who had taken on HUAC, Mississippi racists, Senator Knowland, and the East Bay business community were not about to be denied their rights by the likes of Clark Kerr. Groups representing [liberal student group] SLATE members, anti-HUAC demonstrators, civil rights militants, and ordinary students, some of them conservative, protested the university's actions.

On September 29 the demonstrators defiantly set up tables on the Bancroft strip and refused to leave when told to do so. The next day university officials took the names of five protesters and ordered them to appear for disciplinary hearings that afternoon. Instead of five students, five hundred, led by Mario Savio, marched to Sproul Hall, the administration building, and demanded that they be punished too. Three leaders of the march were added to the list of offenders, and all eight were suspended.

Student Rebellion Begins

The event that converted protest into rebellion occurred on October 1. As students arrived for classes that morning they were greeted by handbills declaring that if they allowed the administration to "pick us off one by one . . . , we have lost the fight for free speech at the University of California." Soon after, . . . other groups set up solicitation tables in front of Sproul Hall, the administration building. At 11:00 A.M. the assistant dean of students . . . asked [campus activist] Jack Weinberg to identify himself.

Weinberg refused, and the dean ordered campus police to arrest him. A veteran of the civil rights movement, Weinberg went limp in standard civil disobedience mode when the guards carried him to a waiting car. Bystanders and observers quickly came to his rescue. In minutes hundreds of protesters, singing the civil rights anthem, "We Shall Overcome," and chanting, "Let him go! Let him go!" surrounded the car, preventing it from leaving to cart Weinberg off to security headquarters.

For the next thirty-two hours Weinberg and his police escort remained captive in the car while speaker after speaker climbed atop the vehicle to address the growing crowd. Savio, here and later the most civil of militants, removed his shoes so as not to damage the police car. He compared the protesters to [American author] Henry David Thoreau, who had briefly defied the authorities to protest the Mexican War that would enlarge United States slave territory. He was followed by other speakers, who were pelted with eggs and lighted cigarettes by about one hundred fraternity brothers and athletes.

The standoff ended with an agreement between Kerr and the warring parties that submitted to a committee of faculty, students, and administrators all issues of campus political behavior and

Student protests took place across the United States in the 1960s. Here, demonstrators sing "We Shall Overcome."

turned over to an academic senate committee the question of sus-
pending the eight students. Weinberg would be released without
charges.

Free Speech Movement Is Born

But the rebellion had only begun. A new organization, the Free
Speech Movement (FSM), was formed with a large executive
committee representing its constituent campus organizations. Despite the FSM's growing fear that the administration was not
dealing with the students in good faith, the next few weeks were
relatively quiet on campus. Yet incidents were accumulating that
would provoke the students and help trip off another confrontation. Berkeley's chancellor Edward Strong refused a request that
he reinstate the eight suspended students while the senate committee deliberated their fate. Kerr, who dismissed the FSM as "a
ritual of hackneyed complaints," failed to realize that faculty,
graduate students, teaching assistants, and undergraduates alike
would perceive the issue as amounting not to how many restrictions had been removed but how many remained. Here the liberalism of the Berkeley administration, disposed to compromise,
crashed head-on into the moral objectives of the student movement, as the liberalism of Kennedy and Johnson collided with
the visionary purity of the civil rights activists.

The FSM proposed that the freedom defined in the First
Amendment be considered the only guide to political activity on
campus. Savio denounced a compromise reached by the senate
committee for imposing prior restraint on student actions. On November 9, in defiance of the administration, Savio and his allies
once again set up literature and solicitation tables. As a prelimi-
nary to disciplinary action, campus police took the names of
seventy-five students supervising the tables. Now the student
movement had antagonized not only the administration but also
many of the more conservative student groups. On the other hand,
it was gaining support among graduate students, many of whom
were poorly paid, overworked teaching assistants [TAs]. The
graduate student organization declared that it would preside over
tables. The administration, the TAs said, would not dare suspend
them since their role was vital to the university's functioning.
They were right. When almost two hundred graduate students set
up tables nothing happened. Many undergraduates, deciding that
the administration was choosing to pick only on the weak, shifted

back to the FSM. What the incident really proved was that in a university essentially liberal in structure, students who were also teachers could undermine administrative authority.

Joan Baez Sings

On November 13 the dilatory liberals on the faculty senate committee finally made a report. Six of the eight suspended students should be reinstated; Savio and Art Goldberg should be kept on suspension for six weeks. By what one administrator described as a "mealy-mouthed liberal nondecision," Savio and Goldberg's sentences, however, should be made retroactive to the incident, more than six weeks in the past. With that problem out of the way, focus returned to the question of campus advocacy and solicitation for off-campus causes. The FSM leaders decided to confront the university's Board of Regents, who were scheduled to meet on the campus on November 20. To assure a good turnout, movement leaders prevailed on Joan Baez, the popular folk singer and a sympathizer with the FSM, to give a free concert during the meeting.

Baez brought out the crowd. Three thousand students gathered near Sproul during the Regents' meeting to listen to speeches. They then snake-danced their way to the west gate of the campus and sat on the grass to hear the singing and await the results of the meeting. The results disappointed most of Berkeley's students. No campus facilities could be used to further causes deemed "unlawful," and the Regents overruled the faculty and increased the punishments on Savio and Goldberg. The student militants could have wondered, like the SNCC [Student Nonviolent Coordinating Committee] workers in Mississippi in their dealings with liberal Democratic party forces in Washington: just what did the establishment want?

Graduate Students Strike

In the few remaining weeks of the semester, the FSM won increasing support on the Berkeley campus. Among administration blunders that brought the militants success was Chancellor Strong's against Savio and his associates for unlawfully hindering campus police from performing their duties. The graduate students decided to go on strike. On Wednesday, December 2, from four to five thousand people, spectators as well as FSM partisans, gathered around Sproul Plaza.

In his indictment of the alienating, impersonal machine that he believed the university had become, Savio found his own authentic eloquence. Martin Luther King in the "Letter from a Birmingham Jail" had spoken of "direct action, whereby we would present our very bodies as a means of laying our case before the conscience of the . . . community." Now Savio announced:

> There's a time when the operations of the machine becomes so odious, makes you so sick at heart, that you can't take part; you can't even passively take part. And you've got to put your bodies upon the gears and upon the wheels, upon the levers, upon all the apparatus, and you've got to indicate to the people who own it that unless you're free, the machines will be prevented from working at all.

This is poetry that combines the exaltation of the civil rights movement with the splendor of the existential vision. It moved the listeners. And it placed the Free Speech Movement at about the point in the spectrum that much of the student left then spoke from: with no suggestion of violence, thinking of concrete change, its discourse as yet unthickened by dogmatic pseudorevolutionary verbiage.

Police Action Taken

Soon after the demonstration in the plaza, student supporters began to fan up and out across four floors of Sproul Hall singing "We Shall Overcome" and Bob Dylan's "The Times They Are-a Changin'." Savio, Weinberg, and others urged people on the plaza to join the sit-in. From one thousand to fifteen hundred went inside the building.

For a time it looked as though the administration would not act. Late that afternoon, university officials declared the building closed and sent employees home. As hours passed and nothing further happened, students inside Sproul relaxed. The FSM leaders designated separate areas and floors for special activities. There was a room for movies, another for a Spanish class, an area for quiet study, and a spot for square dancing.

But off campus the forces of the establishment began to stir. To some observers the Berkeley rebellion seemed a heinous violation of the rules of university decorum, an outrageous defiance of rules and procedures by a privileged group of young people, beneficiaries of a generous taxpaying public. Around midnight the deputy district attorney of Alameda County told Governor Pat Brown in Los Angeles over the phone that "temporizing would only make the eventual blow-off more dangerous." Brown gave permission for the police to move in. Shortly after 2:00 A.M., six hundred California highway patrolmen and Alameda County sheriff's deputies cordoned off Sproul Hall. In the middle of the night Chancellor Strong appeared with a bullhorn admonishing students to leave the building. The Free Speech leaders now began spreading the word that students should go limp to slow down the removal process. That way, the bust would still be going on at the time classes resumed in the morning, and uncommitted students, on the way to lectures and labs, would observe the cops manhandling their fellow students.

The police charged with resisting arrest any student who went limp. At first removals were gentle. Then, as the police tired, they became less careful. They twisted some arms and banged some students' heads on the stairs as they were dragged out. Such treatment by police of students was still an unfamiliar experience. In all it took twelve hours to clear the building, but by midafternoon 773 of the occupiers had been arrested and booked for trespassing. Most were shipped off to the county prison farm at Santa Rosa, where a Black Muslim prisoner, Huey Newton, looked on in amazement; all the students were released on bail the following day to return to Berkeley. It had been the largest mass arrest in the history of California.

The Warren Report

Part I by William H. Stringer;
Part II by the Warren Commission

Americans and citizens worldwide were stunned and saddened by the assassination of popular and youthful President John F. Kennedy in Dallas, Texas, on November 22, 1963. The fourth U.S. president to be killed in office, Kennedy's was the first assassination to occur in the age of television.

Within hours of Kennedy being shot, Dallas police arrested Lee Harvey Oswald, the sole suspect in the president's death. Three days later, during a televised prison transfer, viewers watched in horror as onlooker Jack Ruby, a local nightclub owner, shot and killed Oswald.

The assassination of Kennedy and the bizarre circumstances that followed shocked the nation. Some even speculated that the government was involved in the assassination or that it was the result of a domestic or foreign conspiracy. The public demanded not only a criminal investigation, but also a thorough inquiry to rule out a conspiracy and to uncover the complete truth.

In response, President Lyndon B. Johnson established the President's Commission on the Assassination of President Kennedy, also referred to as the Warren Commission. The commission, chaired by Chief Justice Earl Warren, consisted of seven men representing the U.S. Supreme Court, Senate, House of Representatives, the Central Intelligence Agency, and the public.

On September 27, 1964, after ten months of intensive investigation, the Warren Commission issued an 888-page report. The controversial

Warren Report was harshly criticized by some and strongly defended by others.

The central finding of the commission was that one man, Lee Harvey Oswald, had killed the president. The report refuted speculation that the assassination was part of a domestic or foreign conspiracy or that the government had any involvement.

The commission's findings came under attack from those who deemed it a "whitewash." High-profile critic Jim Garrison, a New Orleans district attorney, began an independent inquiry in 1966 based on an assumption that the assassination had resulted from a conspiracy. To this day, many critics do not accept the conclusions of the Warren Report.

The following two articles appeared in the *Christian Science Monitor* on September 28, 1964, the day after the Warren Report was made public. The author of the first article, William H. Stringer, was chief of the Washington bureau of the *Christian Science Monitor.* The second article is a reprinting of selected sections of the Warren Report's "conclusions and recommendations."

I

The report of the President's Commission on the Assassination of President Kennedy declares, after mammoth research and with powerful documentation, that Lee Harvey Oswald was the sole, unassisted, unconspired-with killer of the late President.

Simultaneously the commission criticizes the United States Secret Service for not developing adequate techniques to meet the expanding hazards confronting presidents who must travel, campaign, confer, and speak in the public glare. It proposes that a committee of Cabinet members or the National Security Council review the protective activities of the Secret Service and related agencies, including the Federal Bureau of Investigation, and consider whether to concentrate the safeguarding of the president in a single agency.

Painstaking Testament

A basic, voluminous 888-page illustrated report, flanked by 24 volumes of testimony and appendices, now becomes the painstaking testament for the United States and the world—the evidence that every possible clue and suspicion has been run to ground in an effort to get the full facts on the tragic event, to prove or discount every fantastic rumor.

The commission found no valid evidence to show that the Soviet Government sought the assassination of President Kennedy, or that Oswald had accomplices in Dallas or was hired or encouraged to become a killer agent during his months in the Soviet Union or his trip to Mexico seeking a visa to Cuba.

It found nothing to indicate any link between Oswald and his own killer, night-club owner Jack Ruby.

Rumors Punctured

In fact, virtually all of the fabulous rumors and reports contained in books and documents published since the Dallas tragedy are found groundless in the report.

The commission, headed by the Chief Justice of the United States, Earl Warren, included Sens. Richard B. Russell (D) of Georgia; and John Sherman Cooper (R) of Kentucky; Rep. Hale Boggs (D) of Louisiana; Rep. Gerald R. Ford (R) of Michigan; Allen W. Dulles, former director of the Central Intelligence Agency; and John J. McCloy, New York banker and diplomat.

Not often in modern history has there been such a "white paper" as this report, examining a national tragedy in minute detail, with experts even recreating the fatal gunplay from the upper window of the Texas schoolbook depository building, and tracing the components of the handmade paper bag with which Oswald carried his Italian-made rifle to work that November 22d in 1963.

Commission Thanked

President Johnson, who appointed the commission last Nov. 29, thanked the members for their determination "to tell the whole truth of these terrible events."

"This is our obligation to the good name of the United States of America and to all men everywhere who respect our nation, and above all to the memory of President Kennedy," he said.

In the commission's findings much testimony, hitherto-undisclosed, is released.

For instance Secretary of State Dean Rusk's comment before the commission June 10:

I have seen no evidence that would indicate to me that the Soviet Union considered that it had an interest in the removal of President Kennedy or that it was in any way involved. . . . I think also that although there had been grave differences between Chairman Khrushchev and President Kennedy, there were evidences of a certain mutual respect that had developed over some of the experiences, both good and bad, through which these two men had lived.

I think both of them were aware of the fact that any chairman of the Soviet Union and any president of the United States necessarily bear somewhat special responsibility for the general peace of the world.

Experts' Testimony

There was also, for example, much testimony to show that it was not difficult to hit a rifle target at somewhat less than 100 yards, using a telescopic sight—in short, that one of the most difficult jobs of the Secret Service is in protecting the president from "someone with a rifle in an upper window."

Ronald Simmons, chief of the ballistics-research laboratory of the Army's infantry-weapons-evaluation branch, testified.

"In order to achieve three hits, it would not be required that a man be an exceptional shot. A proficient man with this weapon, yes."

Robert A. Frazier, FBI firearms expert, said: "From my own experience in shooting over the years, when you shoot at 175 or 260 feet, which is less than 100 yards, with a telescopic sight, you should not have any difficulty in hitting your target."

Hence, on a sunny noon in Dallas, Lee Oswald, a former marine with a "sharpshooter" qualification, watched from a window and was able to hit his target with a Mannlicher-Carcano Italian rifle—bought from a mail-order house in Chicago under no restrictions whatsoever. Nor has Congress yet imposed new restrictions on the easy ordering of guns from mail-order houses.

What were Oswald's motivations?

As traced by the commission, this man who had lived in an orphan asylum, whose mother had struggled for a living, who had never been able to develop a satisfactory contact with his fellow humans or find meaningful activity, had developed a strong hostility "toward every society in which he lived."

In September 1964, after ten months of investigation, the Warren Commission issued a report on the Kennedy assassination.

Oswald evidently wanted to carve a notorious niche in history, as evidence by his earlier attempt to kill Gen. Edwin A. Walker with a bullet which just missed the right-wing advocate as he sat in his Dallas study. Killing President Kennedy has given Oswald the niche he apparently sought.

Then there was "his avowed commitment to Marxism and communism, as he understood the terms"—despite the fact that Moscow found him to be a mercurial, querulous character who would hardly have made a reliable secret agent.

The commission declares that Oswald's outlook "was expressed by his antagonism toward the United States, by his defection to the Soviet Union, by his failure to be reconciled with life in the United States even after his disenchantment with the Soviet Union, and by his effort, though frustrated, to go to Cuba."

Called a "Loner"

"Each of these," the commission report concludes, "contributed to his capability to risk all in cruel and irresponsible actions."

So Lee Oswald is established, in this report, as a "loner," rejecting even the calming attentions of his Russian-born wife, Marina.

The report delves in detail into the assassination itself discussing the various possibilities as to which combination of the three bullets fired might have hit President Kennedy and Gov. John B. Connally of Texas, who was severely wounded. The conclusion is that the first bullet to strike the President, hitting in the neck, would not have been fatal. Perhaps this same bullet unspent, also injured Governor Connally.

But bullet No. 2 or 3, striking the skull, was fatal to the President. No shots could have been fired from any other direction; at least the commission proved this to its satisfaction by tracing trajectories, by noting that the windshield of the presidential car was nicked on the inside (meaning a bullet from the rear), and by testimony of bystanders.

Sightings Reported

Several bystanders said they saw the man with a gun in the window.

The bubble top of the presidential car had been laid aside, on the sunny day, but if in place it would have obstructed only the aim of the assassin, not the bullet, for its plastic was not at all bulletproof.

The commission probed the later shooting of Oswald by Ruby, and concluded there was no relationship between the two, or between Ruby and Officer J.D. Tippit, who was killed by a fleeing Oswald. Rumors had suggested that Oswald and Tippit and Ruby, in some combination, were in collusion.

Ruby's emotional response to the news of President Kennedy's assassination, his closing of his night club, his erratic movements, are all chronicled.

"Ruby has shown no reluctance to answer any questions addressed to him," the commission reports. "The accounts provided by Ruby are consistent with evidence available to the commission from other sources."

Nor did the commission find any evidence to support the speculation or the statements by Oswald's mother that Oswald was an agent, employee or informer of the FBI, the Central Intelligence Agency, or any other United States agency.

Agencies Criticized

But the commission does criticize the governmental agencies for their failure to provide better presidential protection.

Specifically it believes that the FBI should have alerted the Secret Service to Oswald's history and his presence in Dallas.

The Secret Service and FBI differed, before the commission, as to whether Oswald fell within the category of "threats against the president" which should be referred to the service.

The commission concludes that the FBI "took an unduly restrictive view of its role in preventive intelligence work prior to the assassination." Nor have the federal agencies made sufficient use of modern data-processing methods for keeping tabs on potentially dangerous individuals, the commission said.

Roles Held Ill Defined

The advance preparations made in Dallas by the Secret Service also are criticized. The respective responsibilities of local police officials were ill defined, the report said. Nor did the Secret Service check or cause to be checked any buildings located along the motorcade route taken by the President. Responsibility for observing windows was divided between police stationed along the streets and Secret Service agents riding in the motorcade.

Criticized also were the arrangements for Secret Service agents riding in and behind the presidential car. Despite these criticisms, President Johnson presently campaigns in and out of the presidential automobile in a manner that renders Secret Service protection exceedingly difficult.

Finally, the commission notes that the assassination of a president is not a federal crime—though conspiracy to injure a federal officer is such a crime. The commission suggests that Congress remedy this gross deficiency, and that a high-level commission should get at the crucial business of reviewing and overseeing the safety of the president.

II

Following are summary, excerpts from the conclusions, and recommendations of the report by the President's Commission on the Assassination of President John F. Kennedy:

Summary

The assassination of John Fitzgerald Kennedy on Nov. 22, 1963, was a cruel and shocking act of violence directed against a man, a family, a nation, and against all mankind. A young and vigorous leader whose years of public and private life stretched before him was the victim of the fourth presidential assassination in the history of a country dedicated to the concepts of reasoned argument and peaceful political change.

This commission was created on Nov. 29, 1963, in recognition of the right of people everywhere to full and truthful knowledge concerning these events. This report endeavors to fulfill that right and to appraise this tragedy by the light of reason and the standard of fairness.

It has been prepared with a deep awareness of the commis-

Lee Harvey Oswald, above, the sole suspect in Kennedy's death, was shot three days after his arrest, by Jack Ruby, a local nightclub owner.

sion's responsibility to present to the American people an objective report of the facts relating to the assassination.

Conclusions

This commission was created to ascertain the facts relating to the preceding summary of events and to consider the important questions which they raised. The commission has addressed itself to this task and has reached certain conclusions based on all the available evidence.

No limitations have been placed on the commission's inquiry; it has conducted its own investigation, and all government agencies have fully discharged their responsibility to cooperate with the commission in its investigation.

These conclusions represent the reasoned judgment of all members of the commission and are presented after an investigation which has satisfied the commission that it has ascertained the truth concerning the assassination of President Kennedy to the extent that a prolonged and thorough search makes this possible.

Oswald to Blame

1. The shots which killed President Kennedy and wounded Governor Connally were fired from the sixth-floor window at the southeast corner of the Texas Schoolbook Depository. . . .

2. The weight of the evidence indicates that there were three shots fired.

3. Although it is not necessary to any essential findings of the commission to determine just which shot hit Governor Connally, there is very persuasive evidence from the experts to indicate that the same bullet which pierced the President's throat also caused Governor Connally's wounds. However, Governor Connally's testimony and certain other factors have given rise to some difference of opinion as to this probability, but there is no question in the mind of any member of the commission that all the shots which caused the President's and Governor Connally's wounds were fired from the sixth-floor window of the Texas Schoolbook Depository.

4. The shots which killed President Kennedy and wounded Governor Connally were fired by Lee Harvey Oswald. . . .

5. Oswald killed Dallas police patrolman J.D. Tippit approximately 45 minutes after the assassination. This conclusion upholds the finding that Oswald fired the shots which killed President Kennedy and wounded Governor Connally. . . .

6. Within 80 minutes of the assassination and 35 minutes of the Tippit killing Oswald resisted arrest at the theater by attempting to shoot another Dallas police officer.

7. The commission has reached the following conclusions concerning Oswald's interrogation and detention by the Dallas police:

A. Except for the force required to effect his arrest, Oswald was not subjected to any physical coercion by any law-enforcement officials. He was advised that he could not be compelled to give any information and that any statements made by him might be used against him in court. He was advised of his right to counsel. He was given the opportunity to obtain counsel of his own choice and was offered legal assistance by the Dallas Bar Association, which he rejected at the time.

B. Newspaper, radio, and television reporters were allowed uninhibited access to the area through which Oswald had to pass when he was moved from his cell to the interrogation room and other sections of the building, thereby subjecting Oswald to harassment and creating chaotic conditions which were not conducive to orderly interrogation or the protection of the rights of the prisoner.

C. The numerous statements, sometimes erroneous, made to the press by various local law-enforcement officials, during this period of confusion and disorder in the police station, would have presented serious obstacles to the obtaining of a fair trial for Oswald. To the extent that the information was erroneous or misleading, it helped to create doubts, speculations, and fears in the mind of the public which might otherwise not have risen.

Conspiracy Discounted

8. The commission has reached the following conclusions concerning the killing of Oswald by Jack Ruby on Nov. 24, 1963:

A. Ruby entered the basement of the Dallas Police Department shortly after 11:17 A.M. and killed Lee Harvey Oswald at 11:21 A.M.

B. Although the evidence on Ruby's means of entry is not conclusive, the weight of the evidence indicates that he walked down the ramp leading from Main Street to the basement of the police department.

C. There is no evidence to support the rumor that Ruby may have been assisted by any members of the Dallas Police Department in the killing of Oswald.

D. The Dallas Police Department's decision to transfer Oswald to the county jail in full public view was unsound. The arrangements made by the police department on Sunday morning, only a few hours before the attempted transfer, were inadequate.

Of critical importance was the fact that news media representatives and others were not excluded from the basement even after the police were notified of the threats to Oswald's life. These deficiencies contributed to the death of Lee Harvey Oswald.

9. The commission has found no evidence that either Lee Harvey Oswald or Jack Ruby was part of any conspiracy, domestic or foreign, to assassinate President Kennedy. . . .

10. In its entire investigation the commission has found no evidence of conspiracy, subversion, or disloyalty to the United States Government by any federal, state, or local official.

11. On the basis of the evidence before the commission it concludes that Oswald acted alone. Therefore, to determine the motives for the assassination of President Kennedy, one must look to the assassin himself.

Clues to Oswald's motives can be found in his family history, his education or lack of it, his acts, his writings, and the recollections of those who had close contacts with him throughout his life.

The commission has presented with this report all of the background information bearing on motivation which it could discover. Thus, others may study Lee Oswald's life and arrive at their own conclusions as to his possible motives. . . .

Secret Service and FBI

12. The commission recognizes that the varied responsibilities of the President require that he make frequent trips to all parts of the United States and abroad. Consistent with their high responsibilities Presidents can never be protected from every potential threat.

The Secret Service's difficulty in meeting its protective responsibility varies with the activities and the nature of the occupant of the office of President and his willingness to conform to plans for his safety. In appraising the performance of the Secret Service it should be understood that it has to do its work within such limitations. Nevertheless, the commission believes that recommendations for improvements in presidential protection are compelled by the facts disclosed in this investigation. . . .

Although the FBI, in the normal exercise of its responsibility, had secured considerable information about Lee Harvey Oswald, it had no official responsibility, under the Secret Service criteria existing at the time of the President's trip to Dallas, to refer to the Secret Service the information it had about Oswald.

The commission has concluded, however, that the FBI took an unduly restrictive view of its role in preventive intelligence work prior to the assassination. A more carefully coordinated treatment of the Oswald case by the FBI might well have resulted in bringing Oswald's activities to the attention of the Secret Service. . . .

Recommendations

Prompted by the assassination of President Kennedy, the Secret Service has initiated a comprehensive and critical review of its total operations. As a result of studies conducted during the past several months, and in cooperation with this commission the Secret Service has prepared a planning document dated Aug. 27, 1964, which recommends various programs considered necessary by the service to improve its techniques and enlarge its resources.

The commission is encouraged by the efforts taken by the Secret Service since the assassination and suggests the following recommendations:

1. A committee of Cabinet members, including the Secretary of the Treasury and the Attorney General, or the National Security council should be assigned the responsibility of reviewing and overseeing the protective activities of the Secret Service and the other federal agencies that assist in safeguarding the President. . . .

2. Suggestions have been advanced to the commission for the transfer of all or parts of the presidential protective responsibilities of the Secret Service to some other department or agency. The commission believes that if there is to be any determination of whether or not to relocate these responsibilities and functions, it ought to be made by the Executive and the Congress, perhaps upon recommendations based on studies by the previously suggested committee.

3. Meanwhile, in order to improve daily supervision of the Secret Service within the Department of the Treasury, the commission recommends that the Secretary of the Treasury appoint a special assistant with the responsibility of supervising the Secret Service. This special assistant should have sufficient stature and experience in law enforcement, intelligence, and allied fields to provide effective continuing supervisions and to keep the secretary fully informed regarding the performance of the Secret Service. . . .

4. The commission recommends that the Secret Service completely overhaul its facilities devoted to the advance detection of potential threats against the President. . . .

5. The commission recommends that the Secret Service improve the protective measures followed in the planning and conducting of presidential motorcades. In particular, the Secret Service should continue its current efforts to increase the precautionary attention given to buildings along the motorcade route.

6. The commission recommends that the Secret Service continue its recent efforts to improve and formalize its relationships with local police departments in areas to be visited by the President.

7. The commission believes that when the new criteria and procedures are established, the Secret Service will not have sufficient personnel or adequate facilities. The commission recommends that the Secret Service be provided with the personnel and resources which the service and the Department of the Treasury may be able to demonstrate are needed to fulfill its important mission.

8. Even with an increase in Secret Service personnel, the protection of the President will continue to require the resources and cooperation of many federal agencies. The commission recommends that these agencies, specifically the FBI, continue the practice as it has developed, particularly since the assassination, of assisting the Secret Service upon request by providing personnel or other aid, and that there be a closer association and liaison between the Secret Service and all federal agencies.

9. The commission recommends that the President's physician always accompany him during his travels and occupy a position near the President where he can be immediately available in case of any emergency.

No Clear Jurisdiction

10. The commission recommends to Congress that it adopt legislation which would make the assassination of the President and Vice-President a federal crime. A state of affairs where United States authorities have no clearly defined jurisdiction to investigate the assassination of a President is anomalous.

11. The commission has examined the Department of State's handling of the Oswald matters and finds that it followed the law throughout. However, the commission believes that the department in accordance with its own regulations should in all cases

exercise great care in the return to this country of defectors who have evidenced disloyalty or hostility to this country or who have expressed a desire to renounce their American citizenship and that when such persons are so returned, procedures should be adopted for the better dissemination of information concerning them to the intelligence agencies of the government.

12. The commission recommends that the representatives of the bar, law-enforcement associations, and the news media work together to establish ethical standards concerning the collection and presentation of information to the public so that there will be no interference with pending criminal investigations, court proceedings, or the right of individuals to a fair trial.

The 1964 Election: Johnson, Goldwater, and "The Daisy Advertisement"

By Kathleen Hall Jamieson

Democratic president Lyndon B. Johnson, who had assumed the presidency in 1963 following President Kennedy's assassination, beat Republican opponent Barry Goldwater by a landslide in the 1964 presidential election. In the first issue-based election since 1932, voters had a chance to choose from two candidates with radically different ideas and personalities.

Johnson, the incumbent, had fantastic approval ratings because of the good economy and his legislative successes. He was also a master at manipulating the press and went to great lengths to forge a positive relationship with reporters so that they would present him to the public in the best light—as a moderate liberal and peacemaker.

Goldwater, on the other hand, was a staunch conservative and his extreme right-wing ideology had alienated the more moderate members of the Republican Party. He was far from being popular.

With a large number of Republicans already at odds with their candidate, the Johnson campaign strategy was to deepen the divide. According to Goldwater, his statements regarding "extremism in the defense of liberty" were meant as a defense of conservatism. However,

Kathleen Hall Jamieson, *Packaging the Presidency: A History and Criticism of Presidential Advertising*. New York: Oxford University Press, 1984. Copyright © 1984 by Kathleen Hall Jamieson. Reproduced by permission of the publisher.

many people thought they reflected Goldwater's earlier comments about the possible use of nuclear weapons in ending the Vietnam War.

The stage was set for "The Daisy Advertisement," probably the most controversial political commercial of all time. The ad featured a little girl, standing in a field picking daisy petals. Suddenly there was an explosion followed by a mushroom cloud. Next, a poem was quoted and finally there was an appeal to vote for Lyndon Johnson. The ad preyed on the public's fear, implying that if Goldwater won the election he might be willing to set off a nuclear war.

The "Daisy Ad" was considered so controversial that it ran only once—September 7. However, news coverage of the ad perpetuated its message. Goldwater himself never directly responded to the ad that set the tone for the campaign.

Kathleen Hall Jamieson, an expert on political campaigns, is professor of communication and dean of the Annenberg School for Communication at the University of Pennsylvania. In her 1984 book, *Packaging the Presidency*, from which the following excerpts are taken, she discusses the Johnson versus Goldwater election campaign.

The oblique fashion in which the Democrats argued that Goldwater was more likely than Johnson to start a nuclear war or use nuclear weapons in an existing war whispered their fear that such a claim might be dismissed out of hand as unbelievable or worse as believable but so disquieting that the audience is moved to shoot the messenger who carried it.

The Controversial Ad

The most controversial ad aired in 1964 and arguably the most controversial ad in the history of political broadcasting never mentions either Goldwater's name or any statement he has made about anything. It opens on a female child dressed in a jump suit standing in an open field plucking the petals from a daisy as she counts "1,2,3,4,5,7,6,6,8,9." The authenticity of the child derives in large part from the fact that she counts as children do—with numbers out of proper order. She sounds like a child because she counts like a child, a testament to the talents of Tony Schwartz who created the conjoined countdowns. When she reaches "9," a Cape Canaveral voice begins a countdown of its own—no longer innocent but ominous. Here is the efficient, straightforward, willful act of an adult: "10,9,8,7,6,5,4,3,2,1, zero." At zero the camera, which throughout this second countdown has been closing on the child's face, dissolves from her eye to a mushroom cloud that expands until it envelops the screen. Lyndon Johnson's voice is heard stating a lesson that could be drawn from the Sermon on the Mount: "These are the stakes. To make a world in which all of God's children can live, or to go into the dark. We must either love each other or we must die."

The history of this ad has been amply replayed. Projecting their predispositions into the ad, audiences remembered hearing Goldwater's name and a specific attack on his policies when neither was actually in the ad itself. Tony Schwartz, who conceived the idea for the ad and produced its sound track, explains: "It was comparable to a person going to a psychiatrist and seeing dirty pictures in a Rorschach pattern. The Daisy commercial evoked [as its responsive chord] Goldwater's pro-bomb statements. They were like the dirty pictures in the audience's mind." The ad was aired only once on "Monday Night at the Movies" on September 7. . . .

"What is amusing now but wasn't then," says Goldwater's strategist Charles Lichenstein, "is that we gave the daisy ad so much publicity that it was shown over and over on news and commentary programs so a lot of people saw it who wouldn't have ordinarily seen it. We thought it was very damaging so obviously we demanded that it be withdrawn." On behalf of the Goldwater campaign, Dean Burch filed a complaint with the Fair Campaign Practices Committee. "This horror-type commercial is designed to arouse basic emotions and has no place in campaign. I demand you call on the President to halt this smear attack on a United States Senator and the candidate of the Republican party for the Presidency," said Burch. But the Republican protests were rendered moot when the Democrats quickly announced that they would not again air the ad.

Subsequent Ads Incite Fear

The Daisy commercial was not the only ad played a single time but etched into the public consciousness by subsequent discussion and replay. In the second ad, aired on "Saturday Night at the Movies," September 12, a young girl is intently licking an ice cream cone. No exploding bombs will menace her activity. The danger that menaces this child is invisible. Even as it poisons her, she cannot taste the Strontium 90. But as the ad progresses we learn that thanks to the test-ban treaty the child can eat the ice cream without risk. But Goldwater opposed the treaty. So "if he's elected, they might start testing all over again."

The narrative is delivered by a soothing maternal voice, which may be the first use of female voiceover in a political ad. The female announcer reminds the child and us that by voting against the test-ban treaty Goldwater, in effect, endorsed Strontium 90 in the air and food. "Now there's a man who wants to be president of the United States and he doesn't like this treaty. He even voted against it. He voted to go on testing more bombs. His name is Barry Goldwater." But although the female voice is allowed to deliver the voiceover, the ad reverts to the supposedly more authoritative male voice to intone the usual tag.

The fears reflected in the ice cream cone ad mirrored public sentiment. "The big issue in the country was Strontium 90," says [Johnson's assistant Bill] Moyers. "Mothers were marching. The dairy industry was greatly concerned. Kennedy had addressed it before his death. That issue played into our hands because Goldwater had called for more nuclear testing."

"They were both brilliantly devised commercials," concludes Lichenstein. "I admire Doyle Dane as skilled professionals for coming up with them. They were much more imaginative than anything we ever did." Goldwater remembers these two ads "with considerable horror." At the time he declared that Americans "are horrified and the intelligence of Americans is insulted by weird television advertising by which this administration threatens the end of the world unless all-wise Lyndon Johnson is given the nation for his very own."

The third ad in this series also used a female voiceover to describe the need for nuclear restraint as a pregnant woman and her daughter are seen strolling idyllically through a lush park. The ad is lyrical. Images of the woman dissolve over the long shots of the two of them. Since no scientific evidence had established that fallout harmed fetuses, Johnson's advisers refused to OK the storyboard. "I remember telling them 'no,' we would never do it," says [Moyers's assistant Lloyd] Wright. "The agency personnel felt so strongly they went out and did it anyway, I saw it in New York and said 'I don't presume to speak for the whole campaign but that will never see the light of day.' Bill [Moyers] and the others agreed. There was no body of evidence indicating that fallout would damage a fetus. Bombs do blow up people so the daisy ad was based in reality but this ad was going beyond the realm of accepted reality. It was straining for scare tactics."

The most dramatic of the anti-nuclear ads is a chilling five minute recreation of successive U.S. and Soviet bomb tests. It was, says Wright, "an attempt to visually portray the burgeoning arms race." The ad, whose sound was created by Tony Schwartz, alternates countdowns in English and Russian. At the end of each countdown a bomb explodes and mushrooms onto the screen as the counterpart countdown begins. One countdown follows another in progressively more rapid succession, until they are tumbling over each other simultaneously. The escalating madness stops as John Kennedy's voice announces that negotiations for the test ban treaty have been concluded, a subtle suggestion that a vote for Johnson is a vote to "Let us Continue," as he had promised we would following the assassination of Kennedy. Johnson's voice follows, reminding us that the test ban treaty has led us closer to peace and reduced the overall level of radioactivity. Then, in a veiled reference to Goldwater, Johnson says "those who oppose agreement to lessen the dangers of war curse the only light that can lead us out of the darkness. As long as I am your president I will work to bring peace to this world and the world of our children."

Wright was initially fearful that the "ad wouldn't hold the audience." The ad's continuing power to sustain audience interest suggests that that fear was misplaced.

In a final televised ad, a bomb explodes on the screen as an announcer suggests that Goldwater's attitude toward nuclear weapons is inappropriately casual. "On October 24, 1963, Barry Goldwater said of the nuclear bomb 'merely another weapon.'" "Merely another weapon?" repeats the announcer incredulously. . . .

By indicting Goldwater for his inclination to "shoot from the hip" and for being "trigger happy," his opponents identified him with a mythic character from the Old West who invited trouble, whose aim was skewed by his impulsiveness, whose judgment was not trustworthy, who shot first and asked questions later. So, in mid-October, on a swing through the West, Johnson said, "We here in the West know how the West was won. It wasn't won by the man on the horse who thought he could settle every argument with a quick draw and a shot from the hip. We here in the West aren't about to turn in our sterling-silver American heritage for a plastic credit card that reads 'Shoot now, pay later.'" The image of the rampaging cowboy had the advantage of personalizing the decision to use nuclear weaponry. . . .

Goldwater's Ineffective Ad Campaign

A look at Goldwater's advertising explains his problem in 1964. Not only did Goldwater fight the campaign on ground that Johnson had chosen but he also magnified rather than downplayed the stands for which Johnson's ads indicted him. In his first paid half hour televised address, aired September 18, Goldwater tried to preempt the charges that he was trigger happy. "No one was happy with the speech," recalls Stephen Shadegg, Goldwater's Regional Director for Western states. "It was defensive, it dealt in generalities, and it opened with Goldwater's repeating the charges his opponents were making, i.e. that he was impulsive, imprudent, and trigger-happy." In the speech Goldwater argued that the Republicans stood for "peace through preparedness. The Republican party is the party of peace—because we understand the requirements of peace, *and because we understand the enemy*," he noted. The speech embodied the "Republican" posture toward Communism in an analogy in which the enemy was "the schoolyard bully." If he is permitted to push you around, "eventually you'll have to fight." But stand up to him and "he'll back down and there will be no fight."

An eight page advertisement in the October issue of *Reader's Digest* titled "Senator Goldwater Speaks Out On the Issues" also stressed "Peace through Strength.". . .

On September 22, [former president Dwight] Eisenhower was called on to certify that Goldwater could be trusted with the presidency. The difficulties of the task were heightened by the fact that during the California primary Eisenhower had written an article for the Republican New York *Herald-Tribune* that seemed to oppose Goldwater's candidacy. The article offered a series of principles describing the ideology of an acceptable nominee. Those principles—support for civil rights and the UN, willingness to probe ways to lower barriers between east and west, avoidance of impulsiveness—seemed point by point to repudiate Goldwater's candidacy. . . .

Consequently, Goldwater's strategists concluded that the public would not find a strong endorsement of Goldwater by Eisenhower convincing, and doubted, moreover, that Eisenhower would deliver a categorical endorsement if one were scripted for him. Accordingly, the Republicans used the forum "to knock down misperceptions about Goldwater" and "to develop a sense that Barry Goldwater was a decent, thoughtful, humane kind of guy." "Everyone knew that Eisenhower was not very enthusiastic about Goldwater," says Lichenstein, who supervised production and editing of the program, "and we felt that it would have been dishonest and not in keeping with Eisenhower's character or image to come on too strong as a pitchman."

In the "Conversation at Gettysburg," filmed at Eisenhower's farm and aired September 22, Ike and Goldwater engaged in a meandering discussion. The film opened with Eisenhower asking, "Well, Barry, you've been campaigning now for two or three weeks, how do you like it? And how does it seem to be going for you?," questions that set the tone of the conversation to follow. Missing was a decisive, unequivocal endorsement by Ike of Goldwater's candidacy. The closest Ike came was in response to Goldwater's assertion that "our" opponents have called us "warmongers." In an answer not only included in the program but edited into a TV ad of its own, Ike said:

> Well, Barry, in my mind this is actual tommyrot. Now, you've known about war, you've been through one. I'm older than you, I've been in more. But, I tell you, no man who knows anything about war is going to be reckless about it. Now, certainly the country recognizes in you a man of integrity, good will, honesty and dedication to his country. You're not going to be doing these things—what do they call it—push the button? I can't imagine anything you would give more careful thought to than the President's responsibility as the Commander-in-Chief of all our armed forces, and as the man conducting our foreign relations. I am sure that with this kind of an approach you will be successful in keeping us on the road to peace.

"The famous 'tommyrot' statement was the climax of the program, the one we were aiming toward," says Lichenstein. "It was a very effective close."

Flawed Endorsement

Still, even in that statement, Ike had not explicitly endorsed Goldwater but rather all men who know anything about war—a field that presumably included Lyndon Johnson. Ike had not said that he recognized Goldwater as a man of integrity and dedication but that the country "certainly" recognized in him these virtues; yet the country's doubts were what the Goldwater campaign was trying to allay in this broadcast. Instead of saying that he knew that Goldwater would give careful thought to his responsibilities as Commander-in-Chief, Ike said that he couldn't imagine anything Goldwater would give more thought to, not a strong recommendation for a candidate suspected by many of speaking before thinking. Finally, Ike noted that with "this approach," which he left undefined, Goldwater would be successful in keeping the country on the road to peace. What Ike said was not as damaging as what he left unsaid.

"The most charitable thing I can say about the film is that it wasn't effective," wrote Goldwater later. A post-election questionnaire sent by Shadegg to the Republican convention delegates found only 20 percent expressing approval of the content of the "Conversation at Gettysburg." So pleased was Lyndon Johnson with the low ratings "Conversation" received that a few days after its airing he shared with newspersons the fact that its competitors, "Petticoat Junction" and "Peyton Place," had earned ratings of 27.4 and 25.0 to "Conversation at Gettysburg" 's 8.6.

The "Conversation" was one of two half hour programs Lichenstein places in the first phase of the advertising on Goldwater's behalf. "At the beginning of the campaign we had a problem of beating back what we regarded as very dangerous misperceptions of certain policies and positions of Senator Goldwater. In that phase the advertising followed those themes." In addition to "Conversation" this phase included "a network half hour program using a question-and-answer technique we had used to great effect in the California primary."

But in Lichenstein's judgment this question-and-answer session, broadcast October 6, was less effective than its predecessor. "People in the campaign thought that it [the California format] wasn't slick enough to be used nationally. In slicking up the techniques [with rear screen projection of the questioners and arty camera work] its urgency and potency were greatly diminished." For example, one question was put by a truck driver whom viewers saw not in his truck but reflected in the truck's rearview mirror. Goldwater's delivery also seemed more stilted in the second program. In the earlier film, Goldwater had only seen and answered the questions in a single dry run before the final take. "In the national program we lost our nerve and over-edited it. It lost all spontaneity," says Lichenstein.

The questions asked in this program had an anti-Johnson edge to them. What could be done about the conflict between China and Russia? asked one. Was the war on poverty working? asked another. After indicting Johnson's policies, Goldwater set in place the Goldwater-Miller alternative. Short ads, using the same format, were also produced and aired later in the campaign.

During this first phase of the advertising campaign, Goldwater tried to put into context the charges raised against him. In one ad he argued, for example, that some had distorted his concern with Communism "to make it appear we are preoccupied with war. There is no greater political lie. I am trying to carry to the American people this plain message. This entire nation and entire world risk war in our time unless free men remain strong enough to keep the peace."

Meanwhile, the tidal wave generated by Goldwater's statement about empowering the commander of NATO [North Atlantic Treaty Organization] to use nuclear weapons dissipated when news reporters confirmed that under both Eisenhower and Kennedy the NATO commander had held such power, a point also made by former Vice-President Nixon. Still lingering, however, was the residual impression, whether correct or incorrect, that Goldwater had recommended that such power reside with "commanders" not "the commander."

Republicans Go on the Offensive

Recognizing that they were on the defensive about Social Security and use of "the bomb," in early October the Republicans "decided to become more affirmative," says Lichenstein, "to go on the offensive and take the battle to Lyndon Johnson, to make him the issue rather than making Senator Goldwater the issue." The new direction was summarized in a seven-page plan titled "Operation Home Stretch: A Public Relations Strategy" written by Lou Guylay and approved by Goldwater's strategy committee on October 11. In the memo Guylay argued that "we have seen a shocking decline in political morality. . . . This has led to crime and violence on the street—a breakdown of law and order—terrorizing our people. Meanwhile in the world arena we have weakened ourselves and permitted our enemy to make gains all over. Our alliances are failing—the war in Vietnam persists. Cuba is a cancer spreading its poison throughout the Americas." Advertising quickly reflected this new direction.

Martin Luther King Jr. Wins Nobel Peace Prize

Part I by Gunnar Jahn;
Part II by Martin Luther King Jr.

The Nobel Peace Prize has been called the greatest honor that can be bestowed. Award creator Alfred Nobel indicated that the prizes for various fields of humanitarian concern should be given to those who "shall have conferred the greatest benefit on mankind." He added that one medal should go to the person who has, "done the most or the best work for fraternity between nations, for the abolition or reduction of standing armies and for the holding and promotion of peace congresses."

On December 10, 1964, thirty-five-year-old Dr. Martin Luther King Jr. received the Nobel Peace Prize. He became the second African American to win the award, and the youngest recipient of the prize in history.

In the 1950s and 1960s, King, a champion for peace and racial equality, led the civil rights movement. He was an advocate of a nonviolent struggle against segregation and won the Nobel Peace Prize for his unwavering commitment to nonviolent means of bringing people together in the pursuit of civil and racial equality.

In Part I of the following selection, the Nobel Peace Prize presentation speech by Gunnar Jahn, chairman of the Nobel Committee, recognizes the exceptional contributions of Dr. King. The speech was delivered to a group of dignitaries, including King Olav V, in the auditorium of Sweden's Oslo University.

Part I: Gunnar Jahn, Nobel Peace Prize presentation speech, Oslo, Sweden, December 10, 1964.
Part II: Martin Luther King Jr., Nobel Peace Prize acceptance speech, Oslo, Sweden, December 10, 1964.

Part II of the following selection is Dr. King's inspirational acceptance speech. King continued to fight for civil rights, gaining himself and the movement the admiration of millions worldwide. His work was tragically cut short in 1968 when an assassin's bullet took his life.

I

Not many years have passed since the name Martin Luther King became known all over the world. Nine years ago, as leader of the Negro people in Montgomery in the state of Alabama, he launched a campaign to secure for Negroes the right to use public transport on an equal footing with whites.

But it was not because he led a racial minority in their struggle for equality that Martin Luther King achieved fame. Many others have done the same, and their names have been forgotten.

Luther King's name will endure for the way in which he has waged his struggle, personifying in his conduct the words that were spoken to mankind:

Whosoever shall smite thee on thy right cheek, turn to him the other also!

Fifty thousand Negroes obeyed this commandment in December, 1955, and won a victory [with the Montgomery Bus Boycott in Alabama]. This was the beginning. At that time Martin Luther King was only twenty-six years old; he was a young man, but nevertheless a mature one. . . .

Spirit of Brotherly Love

Yet even if victory is won in the fight against segregation, discrimination will still persist in the economic field and in social intercourse. Realistic as he is, Martin Luther King knows this. In his book *Strength to Love* he writes:

"The Court orders and federal enforcement agencies are of inestimable value in achieving desegregation, but desegregation is only a partial, though necessary, step towards the final goal which we seek to realize, genuine intergroup and interpersonal living. . . .

But something must touch the hearts and souls of men so that they will come together spiritually because it is natural and right. . . ."

True integration will be achieved by true neighbors who are willingly obedient to unenforceable obligations.

Martin Luther King's unarmed struggle has been waged in his own country; its result has been that an obdurate, centuries-old, and traditional conflict is now nearing its solution.

Is it possible that the road he and his people have charted may bring a ray of hope to other parts of the world, a hope that conflicts between races, nations, and political systems can be solved, not by fire and sword, but in a spirit of true brotherly love? . . .

Nonviolence Is Essential

Today, now that mankind is in possession of the atom bomb, the time has come to lay our weapons and armaments aside and listen to the message Martin Luther King has given us through the unarmed struggle he has waged on behalf of his race. Luther

Martin Luther King Jr., a tireless advocate of civil rights, was gunned down outside his motel in Memphis in 1968.

King looks also beyond the frontiers of his own country. He says:

"More than ever before, my friends, men of all races and nations are today challenged to be neighborly. . . . No longer can we afford the luxury of passing by on the other side. Such folly was once called moral failure; today it will lead to universal suicide. . . .

If we assume that mankind has a right to survive, then we must find an alternative to war and destruction. In our days of space vehicles and guided ballistic missiles, the choice is either nonviolence or nonexistence. . . ."

Though Martin Luther King has not personally committed himself to the international conflict, his own struggle is a clarion call to all who work for peace.

He is the first person in the Western world to have shown us that a struggle can be waged without violence. He is the first to make the message of brotherly love a reality in the course of his struggle, and he has brought this message to all men, to all nations and races.

Today we pay tribute to Martin Luther King, the man who has never abandoned his faith in the unarmed struggle he is waging, who has suffered for his faith, who has been imprisoned on many occasions, whose home has been subject to bomb attacks, whose life and the lives of his family have been threatened, and who nevertheless has never faltered.

To this undaunted champion of peace the Nobel Committee of the Norwegian Parliament has awarded the Peace Prize for the year 1964.

II

Your Majesty, Your Royal Highness, Mr. President, excellencies, ladies and gentlemen: I accept the Nobel Prize for Peace at a moment when twenty-two million Negroes of the United States are engaged in a creative battle to end the long night of racial injustice. I accept this award on behalf of a civil rights movement which is moving with determination and a majestic scorn for risk and danger to establish a reign of freedom and a rule of justice.

Nonviolence Is a Powerful Solution

I am mindful that only yesterday in Birmingham, Alabama, our children, crying out for brotherhood, were answered with fire hoses, snarling dogs, and even death. I am mindful that only yesterday in Philadelphia, Mississippi, young people seeking to secure the right to vote were brutalized and murdered. I am mindful that debilitating and grinding poverty afflicts my people and chains them to the lowest rung of the economic ladder.

Therefore, I must ask why this prize is awarded to a movement which is beleaguered and committed to unrelenting struggle, and to a movement which has not yet won the very peace and brotherhood which is the essence of the Nobel Prize. After contemplation, I conclude that this award, which I receive on behalf of that movement, is a profound recognition that nonviolence is the answer to the crucial political and moral questions of our time: the need for man to overcome oppression and violence without resorting to violence and oppression.

Civilization and violence are antithetical concepts. Negroes of the United States, following the people of India, have demonstrated that nonviolence is not sterile passivity, but a powerful moral force which makes for social transformation. Sooner or later, all the peoples of the world will have to discover a way to live together in peace, and thereby transform this pending cosmic elegy into a creative psalm of brotherhood. If this is to be achieved, man must evolve for all human conflict a method which rejects revenge, aggression, and retaliation. The foundation of such a method is love.

The torturous road which has led from Montgomery, Alabama, to Oslo bears witness to this truth, and this is a road over which millions of Negroes are traveling to find a new sense of dignity. This same road has opened for all Americans a new era of progress and hope. It has led to a new civil rights bill, and it will, I am convinced, be widened and lengthened into a superhighway of justice as Negro and white men in increasing numbers create alliances to overcome their common problems.

We Shall Overcome

I accept this award today with an abiding faith in America and an audacious faith in the future of mankind. I refuse to accept despair as the final response to the ambiguities of history.

I refuse to accept the idea that the "is-ness" of man's present nature makes him morally incapable of reaching up for the eternal "ought-ness" that forever confronts him.

I refuse to accept the idea that man is mere flotsam and jetsam in the river of life, unable to influence the unfolding events which surround him.

I refuse to accept the view that mankind is so tragically bound to the starless midnight of racism and war that the bright day-break of peace and brotherhood can never become a reality.

I refuse to accept the cynical notion that nation after nation must spiral down a militaristic stairway into the hell of nuclear annihilation.

I believe that unarmed truth and unconditional love will have the final word in reality. This is why right, temporarily defeated, is stronger than evil triumphant.

I believe that even amid today's mortar bursts and whining bullets, there is still hope for a brighter tomorrow.

I believe that wounded justice, lying prostrate on the blood-flowing streets of our nations, can be lifted from this dust of shame to reign supreme among the children of men.

I have the audacity to believe that peoples everywhere can have three meals a day for their bodies, education and culture for their minds, and dignity, equality, and freedom for their spirits.

I believe that what self-centered men have torn down, men other-centered can build up.

I still believe that one day mankind will bow before the altars of God and be crowned triumphant over war and bloodshed and nonviolent redemptive goodwill proclaimed the rule of the land. And the lion and the lamb shall lie down together, and every man shall sit under his own vine and fig tree, and none shall be afraid.

I still believe that we shall overcome.

Prize Honors All Who Believe in Peace

This faith can give us courage to face the uncertainties of the future. It will give our tired feet new strength as we continue our forward stride toward the city of freedom. When our days become dreary with low-hovering clouds and our nights become darker than a thousand midnights, we will know that we are living in the creative turmoil of a genuine civilization struggling to be born.

Today I come to Oslo as a trustee, inspired and with renewed dedication to humanity. I accept this prize on behalf of all men who love peace and brotherhood. I say I come as a trustee, for in the depths of my heart I am aware that this prize is much more than an honor to me personally. Every time I take a flight I am always mindful of the many people who make a successful journey possible, the known pilots and the unknown ground crew. You honor the dedicated pilots of our struggle, who have sat at the controls as the freedom movement soared into orbit. You honor, once again, Chief Lutuli of South Africa, whose struggles with and for his people are still met with the most brutal expression of man's inhumanity to man. You honor the ground crew, without whose labor and sacrifice the jet flights to freedom could never have left the earth. Most of these people will never make the headlines, and their names will never appear in Who's Who. Yet, when years have rolled past and when the blazing light of truth is focused on this marvelous age in which we live, men and women will know and children will be taught that we have a finer land, a better people, a more noble civilization because these humble children of God were willing to suffer for righteousness' sake.

I think Alfred Nobel would know what I mean when I say I accept this award in the spirit of a curator of some precious heirloom which he holds in trust for its true owners: all those to whom truth is beauty, and beauty, truth, and in whose eyes the beauty of genuine brotherhood and peace is more precious than diamonds or silver or gold. Thank you.

CHRONOLOGY

January 8: President Lyndon B. Johnson declares a war on poverty during his first State of the Union address.

January 11: The U.S. surgeon general issues the first report showing a causal link between smoking and disease. Several days later the Federal Trade Commission releases new guidelines for cigarette advertising.

January 13: Folk musician Bob Dylan releases his album *The Times They Are A-Changin'*. The title song from the album becomes an anthem for a generation of young people anxious for social and political change.

January 15: Willie Mays signs a contract with the San Francisco Giants for $105,000 per year, making him the highest-paid player in baseball history.

January 20: The album *Meet the Beatles* is released in the United States, setting the stage for the "British Invasion" of rock-and-roll music. The Rolling Stones release their first album in the United States three months later.

January 23: The Twenty-Fourth Amendment to the Constitution, which eliminates poll taxes, becomes law. A number of southern states, including Georgia, Alabama, and Mississippi, did not ratify the amendment.

February 9: The Beatles perform live on *The Ed Sullivan Show.* It was their first U.S. television appearance and it attracted a record 73 million viewers. They appeared again one week later, drawing 70 million viewers.

February 17: The U.S. Supreme Court rules that congressional districts should be roughly equal in population.

February 25: Cassius Clay defeats Sonny Liston to become the world heavyweight boxing champion. Clay, a Black Muslim, changes his name to Muhammad Ali later that year.

February 27: The movie *Dr. Strangelove, or: How I Learned to Stop Worrying and Love the Bomb* is released. Directed by Stanley Kubrick, it is a dark comedy about the evils of nuclear war.

March 13: Queens, New York, resident Kitty Genovese is publicly stabbed to death in an incident that shocks the nation. Her cries for help are unheeded by thirty-eight people who later stated to police that they "didn't want to get involved."

March 14: Jack Ruby is convicted of the murder of Lee Harvey Oswald and sentenced to death.

March 26: The Reverend Dr. Martin Luther King Jr. meets Black Muslim leader Malcolm X, who had recently split with the Black Nation of Islam, for the first and only time.

March 28: The Great Alaska Earthquake, registering an astounding 9.2 on the Richter scale, hits Prince William Sound at 5:36 P.M. Its force is so great that it registers on seismographs around the world. The quake generates a tsunami that kills 110 people along the western coast of the United States, including 12 in California. Because of the event's time and epicenter, the death toll from the earthquake alone was much lower—just 15 lives lost.

April 3: Malcolm X gives his speech "The Ballot or the Bullet" at a symposium in Cleveland, Ohio, sponsored by the Congress of Racial Equality.

April 7: The world of computing changes radically when IBM announces the introduction of the System/360, the first IBM family of compatible machines. Later in the year scientists at Dartmouth College develop BASIC, a programming language, and the American Standard Association adopts ASCII (American Standard Code for Information Interchange) for data transfer.

April 14: Rachel Carson, author of *Silent Spring* and founder of the modern environmental movement, dies of bone cancer.

April 24: The Ku Klux Klan burns crosses at sixty-one locations across Mississippi in one night, giving rise to the historical term *Mississippi Burning*. It was originally used as the FBI code name for investigations into civil rights atrocities of the year.

May 1: The 1964 World's Fair opens at Flushing Meadows in Queens, New York. Ford Motor Company unveils the first Mustang at the fair.

May 18: Bayard Rustin, one of the principal organizers of 1963's March on Washington, leads a one-day boycott of New York public schools to protest racial inequity within the school system.

May 22: In a speech at the University of Michigan, President Johnson announces his intention to expand the war on poverty and create a Great Society of American prosperity.

June 14: Ken Kesey, author of *One Flew Over the Cuckoo's Nest*, and his group of friends, the Merry Pranksters, begin their cross-country trip in a psychedelic school bus. Along the way they visit counterculture guru Timothy Leary and Jack Kerouac, author of *On the Road*.

June 21: Mississippi Freedom Summer activists Michael Schwerner, James Chaney, and Andrew Goodman are reported missing, igniting a massive manhunt and international controversy that brings unwanted attention to the community of Philadelphia, Mississippi.

July 2: President Johnson signs the Civil Rights Act of 1964 into law in a televised address designed to quell racial tensions.

July 13: Arizona senator Barry Goldwater accepts the nomination for president at the Republican Party's National Convention in San Francisco, California.

July 19: Race riots break out in the Harlem neighborhood of New York after an African American teen is killed by a white police officer.

July 28: NASA's *Ranger 7*, an unmanned lunar lander, is launched. Three days later it returns historic pictures of the moon's surface.

August 2 and 4: North Vietnamese torpedo boats allegedly attack the U.S. destroyer *Maddox* in the Gulf of Tonkin.

August 4: The bodies of the three civil rights workers, Michael Schwerner, James Chaney, and Andrew Goodman, are discovered buried in an earthen dam. Chaney, an African American, had been savagely beaten.

August 5: President Johnson asks Congress for a resolution against North Vietnam following the Gulf of Tonkin incident.

August 7: Congress approves the Gulf of Tonkin Resolution, which allows the president to take any necessary measures to repel further attacks and to provide military assistance to any Southeast Asia Treaty Organization (SEATO) member. Senators Wayne L. Morse of Oregon and Ernest Gruening of Alaska cast the only dissenting votes. President Johnson orders the bombing of North Vietnam.

September 4: Congress approves the Wilderness Act of 1964, creating a National Wilderness Preservation System.

September 14: The Kellogg company introduces one of the first convenience foods, Pop-Tarts toaster pastries.

September 18: Martin Luther King Jr. meets Pope Paul VI in Vatican City. The pope pledges his support to the Negro struggle and the civil rights movement.

September 27: The Warren Commission releases its report on the Kennedy assassination. The committee finds Lee Harvey Oswald to be the lone gunman.

October 1: Students at the University of California at Berkeley rally to protest university rules affecting their freedom of speech. The protest continues into the night and several hundred police are called in to disperse the crowd. The Free Speech Movement is officially formed in the following days.

October 12: The Soviets launch *Voskhod I*, the first manned space flight with a crew of three.

October 14: Soviet premier Nikita Khrushchev is deposed, due in part to the events of the Cuban Missile Crisis. Leonid Brezhnev and Aleksey Kosygin take power.

October 15: The St. Louis Cardinals beat the New York Yankees 4-3 to win the World Series.

November 3: President Johnson and vice presidential candidate

Hubert Humphrey win in a landslide victory over Republican challenger Barry Goldwater.

November 18: After Dr. King criticizes the FBI's failure to protect civil rights workers, the agency's director, J. Edgar Hoover, denounces King as "the most notorious liar in the country." A week later he states that the Southern Christian Leadership Conference is "spearheaded by Communists and moral degenerates."

November 28: NASA launches the unmanned *Mariner 4* to explore the surface of Mars. It arrives almost seven months later on July 14, 1965, returns close-up photos of the Martian surface, and then moves into solar orbit.

December 4: Nineteen members of the "Mississippi Burning" conspiracy are arrested and charged with violating the civil rights of the three slain civil rights workers.

December 10: Dr. King receives the Nobel Peace Prize for his work in civil rights at a ceremony in Stockholm, Sweden. He becomes the youngest person to win the prize.

The Civil Rights Movement

Taylor Branch, *Pillar of Fire: America in the King Years, 1963–1965.* New York: Simon and Schuster, 1998.

James A. Geschwender, ed., *The Black Revolt: The Civil Rights Movement, Ghetto Uprisings, and Separatism.* New York: Prentice-Hall, 1971.

James P. Hanigan, *Martin Luther King, Jr. and the Foundation of Nonviolence.* Lanham, MD: University Press of America, 1984.

James Haskins, *Bayard Rustin: Behind the Scenes of the Civil Rights Movement.* New York: Hyperion Press, 1997.

Coretta Scott King, *My Life with Martin Luther King, Jr.* New York: Henry Holt, 1993.

Robert D. Loevy, ed., with contributions by Hubert H. Humphrey, Joseph L. Rauh Jr., and John G. Stewart, *The Civil Rights Act of 1964: The Passage of the Law That Ended Racial Segregation.* Albany: State University of New York Press, 1997.

Paul L. Montgomery, "Night of Riots Began with Calm Rally," *New York Times*, July 20, 1964.

New York Times, "Key Negro Groups Call on Members to Curb Protests; Moratorium Is Sought Until Presidential Vote—More Political Action Urged," July 30, 1964.

Fred Powledge, *Free at Last? The Civil Rights Movement and the People Who Made It.* Boston: Little, Brown, 1991.

———, "Rustin Is Fearful of Violence Here; Says May 18 March Could Help Ease Tension," *New York Times*, May 9, 1964.

Charles Whalen and Barbara Whalen, *The Longest Debate: A Legislative History of the 1964 Civil Rights Act.* Cabin John, MD: Seven Locks Press, 1985.

The Counterculture

Ken Kesey and Ron Bevirt, *The Further Inquiry*. New York: Viking Press, 1990.

Paul Perry, *On The Bus: The Complete Guide to the Legendary Trip of Ken Kesey and the Merry Pranksters and the Birth of the Counterculture*. New York: Thunder's Mouth Press, 1990.

Peter O. Whitmer and Bruce Vanwyngarden, *Aquarius Revisited: Seven Who Created the Sixties Counterculture That Changed America: William Burroughs, Allen Ginsberg, Ken Kesey, Timothy Leary, Norman Mailer, Tom Robbins, and Hunter S. Thompson*. New York: Macmillan, 1987.

Tom Wolfe, *The Electric Kool-Aid Acid Test*. New York: Bantam Doubleday Dell, 1999.

The Free Speech Movement

David Burner, *Making Peace with the Sixties*. Princeton, NJ: Princeton University Press, 1996.

Robert Cohen, Reginald E. Zelnick, and Leon F. Litwack, *The Free Speech Movement: Reflections on Berkeley in the 1960s*. Berkeley: University of California Press, 2002.

David Lance Goines, *The Free Speech Movement: Coming of Age in the 1960s*. Berkeley, CA: Ten Speed Press, 1993.

Wallace Turner, "Berkeley Peace Parley Upset as Police Grab Student," *New York Times*, December 7, 1964.

————, "796 Students Arrested as Police Break Up Sit-In at U of California," *New York Times*, December 3, 1964.

Johnson's Great Society and the War on Poverty

Edwin Cobb, *No Cease Fires: The War on Poverty in the Roanoake Valley*. Cabin John, MD: Seven Locks Press, 1984.

Robert Dallek, *Flawed Giant: Lyndon Johnson and His Times, 1961–1973*. New York: Oxford University Press, 1998.

Robert A. Divine, ed., *The Johnson Years*. Lawrence: University Press of Kansas, 1987.

Marvin E. Gettleman and David Mermelstein, eds., *The Great Society Reader: The Failure of American Liberalism.* New York: Random House, 1967.

E.W. Kenworthy, "President Pitches His Voice Low and His Hopes High," *New York Times*, January 9, 1964.

David Zarefsky, *President Johnson's War on Poverty: Rhetoric and History.* Tuscaloosa, AL: University of Alabama Press, 1986.

Mississippi Freedom Summer

Jinny Glass Mississippi Freedom Summer Diary, University of Southern Mississippi McCain Library and Archives, August 7–25, 1964. www.lib.usm.edu/~archives/m257.htm? m257text. htm~mainFrame.

Doug McAdam, *Freedom Summer.* New York: Oxford University Press, 1988.

Nicolaus Mills, *Like a Holy Crusade: Mississippi, 1964—The Turning of the Civil Rights Movement in America.* Chicago: I.R. Dee, 1992.

Newsweek, "Civil Rights: Fantasy's End," August 17, 1964.

Newsweek, "Mississippi—'Everybody's Scared,'" July 6, 1964.

The 1964 Election

Stephen Ansolabehere and Shanto Iyengan, *Going Negative: How Attack Ads Shrink and Polarize the Electorate.* New York: Free Press, 1995.

Edwin Diamond and Stephen Bates, *The Spot: The Rise of Political Advertising on Television.* Cambridge, MA; London: MIT Press, 1984.

"Johnson: Daisy Girl Video," American Museum of the Moving Image. www.ammi.org/cgi-bin/video/years.cgi?1964,,,,D,.

Stephen C. Shadegg, *What Happened to Goldwater? The Inside Story of the 1964 Republican Campaign.* Austin, TX: Holt, Rinehart, and Winston, 1965.

Theodore White, *The Making of the President, 1964.* Austin, TX: Atheneum, 1965.

Popular Culture

Alfred G. Aronowitz, "The Beatles: Music's Gold Bugs," *Saturday Evening Post*, March 21, 1964.

Hunter Davis, *The Beatles*. New York: W.W. Norton, 1968.

Margot A. Henricksen, *Dr. Strangelove's America: Society and Culture in the Atomic Age*. Berkeley and Los Angeles: University of California Press, 1997.

Richard Lemon, "George, Paul, Ringo, and John," *Newsweek*, February 24, 1964.

Mark Lewisohn, *The Complete Beatles Chronicles*. New York: Harmony Books, 1992.

Robert Lipsyte, "Clay Discusses His Future, Liston, and the Black Muslims," *New York Times*, February 27, 1964.

Mike Marqusee, *Redemption Song: Muhammad Ali and the Spirit of the Sixties*. London: Verso, 1999.

Newsweek, "Direct Hit," February 3, 1964.

David Remnick, *King of the World: Muhammad Ali and the Rise of an American Hero*. New York: Random House, 1998.

Smoking and Health

Advisory Committee to the Surgeon General of the Public Health Service, "Smoking and Health," U.S. Department of Health, Education, and Welfare, January 11, 1964. www.cdc.gov/tobacco/sgr/sgr_1964/sgr64.htm.

B. Davidson, "Crash Effort for a Safer Cigarette," *Saturday Evening Post*, April 18, 1964.

David A. Kessler, *A Question of Intent: A Great American Battle with a Deadly Industry*. New York: Public Affairs, 2001.

Eileen Shanahan, "Health Warning in Cigarette Ads Proposed by F.T.C.," *New York Times*, January 18, 1964.

U.S. News & World Report, "Smokers' Slowdown: How Long Will It Last?" February 24, 1964.

The Tonkin Gulf Incident

The Avalon Project: Tonkin Gulf Incident, Yale School of Law, 1996. www.yale.edu/lawweb/avalon/tonkin-g.htm.

Joseph C. Goulden, *Truth Is the First Casualty: The Gulf of Tonkin Affair: Illusion and Reality.* Chicago: Rand McNally, 1969.

Edwin E. Moise, *Tonkin Gulf and the Escalation of the Vietnam War.* Chapel Hill: University of North Carolina Press, 1996.

Ezra Y. Siff, *Why the Senate Slept.* Westport, CT: Praeger, 1999.

Tom Wells, *The War Within: America's Battle over Vietnam.* Berkeley: University of California Press, 1994.

Websites

Lyndon Baines Johnson Library and Museum, www.lbjlib.utexas. edu. Run by the National Archives and Records Administration, this site features speeches, oral histories, and audio/video clips from the Johnson administration. The "LBJ for Kids" section contains information on President Johnson's Great Society initiatives as well as biographical information, a photo gallery, and interactive quizzes.

The Martin Luther King Jr. Papers Project at Stanford University, www.stanford.edu/group/King. Started by the King Center for Nonviolent Change and run by Stanford University, this website contains comprehensive information about King and his legacy. It includes his speeches, sound clips, and an interactive time line.

Treasures of Congress: Congress and the Civil Rights Act of 1964, www.archives.gov/exhibit_hall/treasures_of_congress/page_ 24.html. This site, also run by the National Archives and Records Administration, contains historical images and photos of original documents. Additional information on American history, including exhibits on 1960s presidents Eisenhower, Kennedy, and Nixon, can be found in the "Exhibit Hall."

The Vietnam War, www.vietnampix.com. Swedish graphic designer and Vietnam historian Peter Leuhusen has created a striking photo essay of the Vietnam War. Images are arranged in the style of a tour that starts with maps and historical background on the war.

INDEX

Advisory Committee to the Surgeon General, 18
Ali, Muhammad, 13
  joins Nation of Islam, 42–43, 44–45
Aptheker, Herbert, 91
Aronowitz, Alfred G., 31
Aspinall, Neil, 38

Babbs, Ken, 75
Baez, Joan, 95
"Ballot or Bullet" speech (Malcolm X), 13–14
Beatles, 14, 31–40
  early days of, 38–39
  U.S. tour of, 40
Bevirt, Ron, 75, 76
Black Muslims, 41
Bremmer, Robert H., 11
Brown, Jim, 42
Brown, Pat, 97
Brown v. Board of Education, 61
Bruce, Lenny, 13
Bundy, William, 87
Burch, Dean, 114
Burner, David, 90
Burton, Jane, 74

Caldwell, Louise, 36
Cannon, Jimmy, 43
Casano, Kathy, 75
Cassady, Neal, 75
Chaney, James, 78, 79, 80
Christian Science Monitor (newspaper), 99
cigarette advertising, FTC restrictions on, 18–19
Civil Rights Act (1964), 11, 65

Clay, Cassius. See Ali, Muhammad
Congress of Racial Equality (CORE), 65
Connally, John B., 103
Cuban Missile Crisis (1962), 27

Dr. Strangelove, or: How I Learned to Stop Worrying and Love the Bomb (film), 27–30
Dukes, Nelson C., 67, 68, 69
Dulles, Allen, 78, 81
Dylan, Bob, 14

Easy Rider (film), 73
Economic Opportunity Act (1964), 47
Ed Sullivan Show (TV series), 14, 31
Eisenhower, Dwight D., 117–18
election, of 1964, 12
  ad campaigns of
    by Goldwater, 117–20
    by Johnson, 113–17
Electric Kool-Aid Acid Test, The (Wolfe), 72
Epstein, Brian, 38

Federal Bureau of Investigation (FBI), criticism of, 103–104, 108–109
Federal Trade Commission (FTC), restrictions on cigarette advertising by, 18–19
Frazier, Robert A., 101
Freedom Summer, 14, 77–82
Free Speech Movement, 90–97
  birth of, 94–95

Gilligan, Thomas, 67
Gilmore, Voyle, 39
Goldberg, Art, 95
Goldwater, Barry, 12, 65–66, 86, 112–13, 115
Goodman, Andrew, 78, 79–80
Great Society, 10–11, 46–52
Green, Marshall, 86
Gruening, Ernest, 15, 83, 89
Guylay, Lou, 120

Harlem Riot, 65–71
Harrison, George, 33, 36–37
Hoover, J. Edgar, 80
House Un-American Activities Committee (HUAC), 90
Humphrey, Hubert, 56

Jahn, Gunnar, 121
Jamieson, Kathleen Hall, 112
Johnson, Lyndon B., 46, 83, 98
  Freedom Summer campaign and, 78, 80, 81, 82
  Great Society program of, 10–11
  Gulf of Tonkin Resolution and, 15, 84–86
  on signing of Civil Rights Act, 53–54
Johnson, Paul B., Jr., 81–82
Jones, Leroy, 44

Kennedy, John F., assassination of, 10, 98
  summary of Warren report on, 104–11
Kennedy, Robert F., 81
Kerr, Clark, 91, 92
Kesey, Ken, 72
King, Martin Luther, Jr., 12, 53, 96, 121
  on nonviolence, 124–25
  receives Nobel Peace Prize, 16, 121–27
Knowland, William, 92
Kubrick, Stanley, 27–30

Ku Klux Klan, 13

Lambrecht, Steve, 74–75
Lennon, Cynthia, 36–37
Lennon, John, 33, 35–36, 38
Lichenstein, Charles, 114, 115, 118, 119, 120
Liston, Sonny, 41, 42
Little, Malcolm. *See* Malcolm X
Los Angeles Times (newspaper), 83
Louis, Joe, 43

Maddox (destroyer), 85, 88
Making Peace with the 60s (Burner), 91
Malcolm X, 13, 41, 91
Markson, Jimmy, 43
Marqusee, Mike, 41
McCarthy, Joseph, 90
McCartney, Paul, 33, 34–35
McNamara, Robert, 84
Merry Pranksters, 72–76
Mississippi Freedom Democratic Party (MFDP), 77
Montgomery, Paul L., 65
Morse, Wayne, 15, 83, 89
Moyers, Bill, 115

New Deal, 10–11
Newsweek (magazine), 27, 77
Newton, Huey, 97
New York Times (newspaper), 66
Nobel Peace Prize, 16

Oakland Tribune (newspaper), 92
Office of Economic Opportunity (OEO), 46, 47
One Flew over the Cuckoo's Nest (Kesey), 72
Oswald, Lee Harvey, 10, 98, 99
  motivations of, 101–102
  Warren report on, 106–107

Packaging the Presidency (Jamieson), 113

Patterson, Floyd, 43
Perry, Paul, 72
Powell, James, 67
Price, Cecil, 80

Rainey, L.A., 80
Reader's Digest (magazine), 117
Redemption Song: Muhammad Ali and the Spirit of the Sixties (Marqusee), 41
Robinson, Jackie, 44
Rolling Stones, The, 14
Roosevelt, Franklin Delano, 10
Rostow, Walt, 86
Ruby, Jack, 10, 98, 103, 107
Rusk, Dean, 85, 87
  on Warren Commission report, 100–101
Russell, Ernest, 68
Rustin, Bayard, 12

Saunders, Charles, 67
Savio, Mario, 91–92, 95, 96
Schuyler, George, 44
Schwartz, Tony, 113, 114, 116
Schwerner, Michael, 78, 79, 80
Secret Service, Warren Commission recommendations for, 109–10
Shedegg, Stephen, 117
Simmons, Ronald, 101
smoking
  health effects of, 19
    cancers, 23–24
    cardiovascular disease, 25
    evidence in, 20–22
    prospective studies on, 22–23
    respiratory disease, 24–25
  psychosocial aspects of, 26
Sometimes a Great Notion (Kesey), 72, 74
Sommerville, Brian, 32
Southeast Asia Resolution (1964). *See* Tonkin Gulf Resolution
Sprowal, Chris, 67
Starr, Ringo, 33–34, 38, 40

Stockdale, James, 84
Stringer, William H., 98
Strong, Edward, 94, 95, 97
Sundsten, Paula, 75

Taylor, Harry, 69
Terry, Luther, 18
Thoreau, Henry David, 93
"Times They Are A-Changing, The" (song), 14–15
Tippit, J.D., 103
Tonkin Gulf incident, 83
  events of, 88–89
Tonkin Gulf Resolution (1964), 15, 84, 89
Turner Joy (destroyer), 88–89

University of California at Berkeley
  Free Speech Movement and, 90–95
  strike of graduate students at, 95–97
urban renewal, 48–50

Vietnam War, 15–16

Walker, Edwin A., 101
Wallace, George C., 13, 53
  on Civil Rights Act, 14
  on press, 57–58
  on Supreme Court, 58–62
War on Poverty, 11
  components of, 46
Warren, Earl, 98
Warren Commission, 98, 99–100
  members of, 100
  recommendation of, 109–11
War Within: America's Battle over Vietnam, The (Wells), 84
Weinberg, Jack, 92–93
Wells, Tom, 83, 84
Wilkins, Roy, 43, 81
Wilson, Woodrow, 51
Wolfe, Tom, 72
Wright, Lloyd, 115